Mark ar

The Ultimate Guide to Build and Grow Your Personal Brand

by Kristine Monaghan

Published by Mabel and Stanley Publishing

1st edition 2024

Disclaimer

The advice offered in this book is based on the author's lived experience and learnings over many years in business and business coaching.

The author cannot in any way be held responsible for, nor guarantee, any results that do or do not arise as a result of acting on the advice given.

Please remember that results will vary considerably from business to business and individual to individual.

Contents

"If someone offers you an amazing opportunity and you're not sure how to do it – say yes and you can learn to do it later." Richard Branson

"I don't like to gamble, but if there's one thing I like to bet on, it's myself." Beyonce Knowles

"Show up – 80% of success is showing up." Grant Cardone

"In learning the art of storytelling by animation, I have discovered that language has an anatomy." Walt Disney

"If you want to be successful, you've got to be willing to use every connection you've got." Magic Johnson

"Hard work will always bring opportunities." Karen Brady

"Never, set limits, go after your dreams. Don't be afraid to push boundaries." Paula Radcliffe

"It's not about how hard you can hit. It's about how hard you can get hit and keep moving forward."

Rocky Balboa

Foreword

For many, 2021 was a time of extremes, as the world continued to grapple with the chaos and pain of the COVID-19 pandemic. For me, it was the year that everything I had worked so hard to build, evaporated, right in front of me. In 2021 I exited two businesses, one that I had built up from scratch over nine tough years -(a children's activity business) and the other, a two-year long attempt to bring a new business concept to the whole of Scotland, that in the end just didn't work out; but that's a story for another day.

Helplessly witnessing the end of both my businesses was definitely not in my life plan. It was sadly, just something that happened. However, with it, came an unexpected but surprisingly welcome relief. Standing at the crossroads, I found myself for the first time in many years, holding a clean slate and an opportunity from the ashes, to create something different, something big, something for myself.

Truth be told, I had actually started mapping out my current business back in 2019, with the aim of launching in 2020, but when the virus hit, my vision got sacked off and was left to sit cooling on the back burner, while I drained myself of energy, desperately trying to save my two businesses from bankruptcy.

That period of time was one of the toughest of my life, and like many business owners I suffered not only financially, but mentally, physically and emotionally too.

Faced with being unintentionally unemployed for the first time in my life, I decided to dig out one of the many notebooks, (that I had sitting on my bookshelf), to start hatching a new plan. I'm a sucker for a pretty notebook, (the more colourful the better), so I'm always buying new ones when I'm out and about. I use them to write down my ideas for life and business, happiness, and success; I've even got a fairly decent bucket list written down across a number of them. So, with well over 10 years of light bulb moments scattered across at least a thousand pages of miniature art, I set to it; there had to be something in there that I could use.

Pre-covid, I had often considered the notion of becoming a business consultant. I liked the idea of flying around the UK, meeting clients in fancy hotels, solving all their problems and then jetting off again, perhaps with my expert team of coaches at my side in true 'A Team' style. However, at the time, life and geography made that particular transition very difficult. Not only did I have two wonderful young daughters at home who needed their mum, (and who I needed just as much), we just so happened to be living on one of the most beautiful islands off the West Coast of Scotland, out in the Atlantic; The Isle of Lismore.

There is a lot to be said for a life of peace and quiet on an island. A place where the air is fresh, drinking water as clear as gin, comes bubbling up out of the ground, the children run free, and where the chicken, sheep, and our sheepdog dachshunds, provide constant entertainment. However, options are limited for a recently jobless, eternal entrepreneur, with itchy feet and a crazy case of perimenopause; that particular clock never stops ticking, one way or another.

So, notebook in hand, looking back over the pages, I was reminded of a fellow entrepreneur that I admired greatly. I came across this particular marketing guru back in 2017 after an advert popped up in my Facebook timeline. Her name was Claire Mitchell, the "Girls Mean Business" woman. The advert was promoting her Marketing Planner, an awesome and extremely pretty hardback book. I was like a moth to a flame, given my particular notebook vice, and I had instantly hit the buy button. It was soon apparent that Claire knew her audience well, and her ideal customer was clearly me*: a female business owner, aged between 25-40 years old, who is potentially feeling overwhelmed with marketing their business, and who also loves pretty stationary.* For me, the timing was perfect. Back then I was determined to make my franchise business a household name, but I knew I needed help with marketing, and Claire had the solution.

I started to follow Claire on the socials; reading the emails that landed in my inbox, listening to her podcasts, and soaking up her pearls of wisdom. I loved being part of her world and inevitably started dipping my toes into her paid products. I started off buying some of her smaller digital courses, taking what I learned and implementing it into my business. It got me results! Things were starting to click into place.

Then she launched a course called. "Six Figure It Out". Of course, it was a dream of mine to hit that six-figure target, it's a dream many of us budding entrepreneurs, seem to share. It's the validation of our status as a business owner. Right? Honestly, I have no idea why we feel we need to hit the 100k mark in order to prove our worth. Yes, 100k is 100k, but I'm sure your accountant will tell you, you need to earn a lot more than 100k to make up for what the VAT will be costing you, in its various forms, as soon as you hit the threshold.

Anyway, back to the point. This new course, "Six Figure It Out", was like a big shiny disco ball! It was all twinkly and sparkly and it sang out, "Buy me, Buy me!" every time I looked at the advert; now that's a sign of great marketing!

The course was all about how to turn the knowledge in my head into digital products. I knew I had a lot of knowledge in my head. I had acquired it from my years in business: recruitment, franchising, accountancy, legals and marketing, all the way through to coaching and building systems and processes. Like I said, I already knew this was all an asset, I just didn't know how to get it all out of my head and turned into meaningful and viable products that I could sell to the people who needed it.

The advertising was clear. Claire was going to show me everything I needed to know, so I hit the button. It was the biggest investment I had ever made in myself, at around £600; it felt like a huge amount of money to spend just on learning and improving myself. The idea of spending that much money on something as ethereal and as intangible as somebody else's knowledge, just so I could learn something new, sounded crazy, but you know what? It was worth every penny. Totally. If only I had recognised then, what I know for a fact now!

Nothing is more valuable in business than the acquisition of knowledge, and the faster you acquire that knowledge, the faster you become a robust business owner.

Fast forwarding four years to 2021, as I sat looking through my notebooks in the search for inspiration, I came across Claire again and the notes that I had painstakingly documented in a particularly nice notebook, along with a reference to a perfectly sculpted mind map in a mind mapping tool called Mindmeister. I booted up the laptop and logged in. Thankfully it was all still there, just waiting for its moment to shine.

A year later, in January 2022, I launched my new enterprise: The Children's Activity Business Club. Over the 10 years of building a national franchise company, I had awarded over 70 franchises, and had a strong network of 40 franchisees just before the pandemic hit. I had also brought a brand-new sports concept to Scotland as a master franchisee and employer, and had taught athletics, (my first love), to hundreds of children weekly across the country. There had been ups and there had been downs, too many to mention, but after reviewing everything I had learned from running those two businesses, and armed with my trusty notebooks, I knew exactly what I needed to do; this time the road to success was going to be smoother.

I devised a way to share the contents of my brain, simply and efficiently, with likeminded people, and that's just what I did. Over the last two years I've worked with over a thousand business owners to unlock their potential to help maximise their income, so that they get to do what they love.

That's also what I aim to do with this book. In time-honoured fashion, as others have done before me and for me, I'm going to share with you my piece of the infinite jigsaw puzzle that is business ownership. I want to share with you how I have marketed myself like a pop star. How I have brought to the world a service, a product, and an online business and how I teach my clients to do this very thing in their own individual businesses.

My ambition is to give you the opportunity to save yourself from making all the same mistakes I made. I want to give you all the good stuff without the bad, all of the happiness without the scars, and ultimately, a solid series of strategies that you can implement quickly and successfully in your own business.

Whether you're just starting a business, or you have an online business or a product already in the market, this book is for you.

Let's get this show on the road!

"If you're not visible, then you're invisible."

Tru Powell

Introduction

So, what does it mean to Market Like a Pop Star?

From a young age, or since the Virgin Tour in 85, I have loved Madonna, she's awesome. I've seen her LIVE five times and I suppose without knowing it, she has been a life-long inspiration of mine; deep down there is a part of me that wants to be just like her.

When I was young, I remember Madonna being everywhere. Billboards, newspapers, magazines, the London Underground and she was always on Top of the Pops, and I loved TOTP! Everywhere I looked, I saw Madonna. She was in movies! She was even on my bedroom wall.

That's what it means to Market Like a Pop Star. It's the ultimate goal of marketing, to find your perfect customer and make them feel that they are seeing you everywhere, and if they are your perfect customer, they will love it. They will revel in your success, and they will want to be part of it and part of your world.

OK, I don't expect your tribe to have your portrait pinned above their beds, or for them to start wearing the same clothes as you or copying your hairstyle, that would be a bit creepy, but you do want them looking for you. You want to be popping up in their socials, in their stories, in their email box, in their online search, on the notice board at the local shop, in conversations at the gym. You want to be talked about! You want to be recommended. It's all about consistency. It's about showing up with your message, day in day out, and getting your message out there and getting heard.

Once you have this conversation rolling, scaling your business becomes so much easier.

And don't worry about being too visible. If people don't like seeing you, or your emails, then they are not your perfect customer, and you're wasting your time worrying about what they think. Remember, the unsubscribe and opt-out options are <u>your</u> tools for trimming the fat and for streamlining and refining your marketing efforts. Don't be upset when people say they are not interested, thank them.

To help make my point, try this one liner from Tru Powel: "*If you're not visible, then you're invisible.*"

I love this quote; It's horribly obvious but thankfully, right now, I have clients telling me that they understand. That they are aiming to show up in my mobile phone every single day and I think it's great to hear, because this is exactly what it's all about!

And I can tell when somebody is Marketing Like A Pop Star. The volume turns up on their messaging and BAM! they are super visible. Reels, timelines, stories, community groups. They are happening and they are now! When I open my phone, they are there. They understand that to make more sales, they need to Market Like A Pop Star.

So, if the above resonates with you - and I assume it does because why else would you be here? - then hurry to the next page and keep reading. I can't turn you into Madonna, there is still only one of her, and I can't promise to make you an international super star, but I can show you how to get a foot on the global stage, and how to begin Marketing Like A Pop Star.

"Whether you think you can, or you think you can't, you're right."

Henry Ford

The Market Like A Pop Star Rules

"Dreams are free.
Goals have a cost.
Time, effort, sacrifice
and sweat.
How will you pay for
your goals?"

Usain Bolt

RULE 1

Get Your Business Foundations Right

You can't build a house on shifting sands, and just like a house, you need solid foundations to build a business. Get it wrong and everything you've worked hard to achieve, could all come tumbling down around you. There are no shortcuts to success. A tree can only keep growing upwards if it puts down roots.

Yes, that's two analogies in one paragraph, but that's because they fit perfectly. Have you ever noticed how flat the roots are of a tree that's been blown over in the wind?

Foundations are one of the first things I cover when I start working with a new client. The comprise the following 5 core business principles:

1. Your reason for being. Your Why. Your Mission statement.
2. Your Values.
3. Your Vision. Your Ambition. Your Dreams.
4. Your Goals and Milestones.

5. Your Plan.

So, let's begin.

Are you sitting comfortably?

Then tell me, what's your ***WHY***?

Everyone has a reason for starting a business. They either want to be rich, or they want to be their own boss. They want to simply do something different with their lives, something less ordinary, or they just want to get out of a job they hate. They want a new challenge or maybe over dinner and a bottle of wine they have an idea; THE idea.

In my case, it was because I had become a mother.

For most of my adult life I'd had a career in sports development. At the age of nine I joined my first athletics club. I was a runner, and I was good. I knew what I wanted, and I knew what made me happy. I wanted a career in sport. Sport was my life.

At the age of fourteen I started coaching the Under 15's girls' team at my athletics club, under the mentorship of my coach, a fantastic man by the name of Jack Bayliss. I learned so much from Jack. He worked with top athletes that represented the country and when he wasn't doing that, he was mentoring me. Jack taught me everything about coaching from how to write training plans to how to get the best out of young athletes. I loved coaching and working with children, and by the age of sixteen I was a Level 1 qualified coach.

I had a purpose. I had my why!

As I grew older, in order to stay in sport, I was given two options: become a P.E teacher, re-join the education system, teach the standard curriculum and go back to school, or get into sports development, which at the time was an exciting and emerging career.

In essence, 'sport development' was the title given to the work done by various groups of people, effective partnerships, working with the government, local authorities, sports clubs, land and venue owners and sometimes also schools in order to promote sport and sporting opportunities throughout the region.

The work of these groups often included initiatives to create and strengthen opportunities for children to participate and work in sport. It is often done through volunteering and coaching training, targeting specific demographics, event management or even fundraising and generally covers the range of sporting levels from entry to elite and the associated performance pathways.

I wanted other children to have a positive experience of sport like I had had. I knew sport sometimes had a bad rep and was largely underrated amongst children, but I had seen firsthand how it could change lives and how it could lead to a lifelong love and participation.

That desire to share my passion became my central focus, my driving force to forging a career within athletics. This young girl from North London was going places!

I worked for a Children's charity in London for two years, before moving to Oldham to take up the role of Athletics Development Officer for the local authority. My time at Oldham was time well spent and it paved the way for me to achieve my dream of working for the National Governing Body of Sport, England Athletics.

England Athletics was where it was at, and it was where I wanted to be. It's the development body, the home of grass roots athletics and running clubs in England. It's where my heroes were created.

I was appointed as Regional Manager for England Athletics for Yorkshire & Humberside in 1998. I worked with athletics clubs, schools, local authority councils and sports coaches, creating athletics performance programmes and activities for children, from the local level right through to county, regionals, and elites. It was an amazing time with some amazing people, and to this day I feel proud to have been a part of our nation's sporting heritage.

Without knowing it, the work I did then, was shaping me to be the franchisor, businesswoman and entrepreneur that I am today.

After many wonderful years at England Athletics, I left to become the director of a social charity in North London, close to where I grew up, but it wasn't until the ripe old age of 36 that I started my own business. That was the year I had my first daughter.

That year was a big year for me. Not only had I given up my work with the charity to have a baby, I also gave up my hustling bustling life in London for a life of fresh air, clean water, mountains and beaches, on the beautiful Isle of Skye.

I had quit my job to move to Skye with my partner and we had agreed I wasn't going back to work. I loved being a first time mum on the island, I really did, but while my family got on with their lives 636 miles away, and my partner spent 15 hours a day working at sea, I was left adrift, after a complicated birth, in the surreal world of power naps, breast feeding, dirty nappies, and endless episodes of Thomas the Tank Engine, while getting far too familiar with Iggle Piggle and Upsy Daisy in the Night Garden (although at times life felt like I was already taking a ride on the Ninky Nonk), and daily trips to the parent and toddler play groups. In short it didn't take me long before I was going lala and I needed stimulation.

Having a baby is a full-time job in its own right, as every parent knows, but I couldn't help feeling like I'd been put out to pasture. I wasn't ready for retirement and deep down I simply needed my financial independence back. I was also already thinking about the future. I needed a strategy. I wanted to work and so I needed a job that would fit around a family life. A job that would allow me to work my own hours, by my own rules. (I had a new why!) How many interviews do you think I would get through with that attitude?

Becoming self-employed was my only real option.

So, armed with a lifetime of sport, I started looking at creating my own children's athletics activity business for under-fives; I still had all my ideas neatly packed away in those notebooks I mentioned earlier! It would have been exactly the right time too, as we were just about to host the Olympic Games in the UK, (the sporting infrastructure of the games was something I had been working on within England Athletics), but despite all of my ideas and timing, life and circumstance railroaded me in a different direction.

However, it just so happens that by then, my eyes had been opened to a world I hadn't even known existed, pre-motherhood... baby and toddler classes. Suddenly finding myself in this strange new world, I was introduced to a multitude of these small businesses, in the early part of my daughter's life. Some I liked, some I didn't, but there was one that I really loved; it was right up my street. It was called 'Make A Mess'. It was a messy play class where the babies and toddlers could just explore. There were no rules, there was no right or wrong way to play. Nobody telling us what to do, just time with my daughter, making a mess, with lots of other parents and children, all having fun. It was fantastic. By then my daughter was seven months old and was always on the move. She wouldn't sit still and so the class was perfect. It was also the only time and place, outside of our home, that I wasn't in constant fear of my daughter picking something up, sticking it in her mouth and choking on it. Everything at the class was edible, and anything that wasn't edible, like the floor, or other children, was simply too big to eat! The vibe was great, it was relaxed, friendly and fun. I liked it, but best of all I liked the owner.

The owner told me she was franchising the business. I didn't even know what a franchise was back then, so off I went to start some research, to find out what franchising was all about. I even took myself off to a franchise expo in Birmingham to learn more. During that time, I started testing the waters by enquiring with quite a few children's activity franchises across the country, but nothing drew me in like the 'Make A Mess' franchise, which was also, funnily enough, being rebranded as 'Mess Around' at that time.

However, despite how much I wanted in, there was a slight snag. The franchisor wasn't selling her area, and I didn't want to buy a territory outside of where I lived, (we lived not far from each other), so I parked 'Make A Mess', my search continued, and my quest for a business I could get my teeth into, carried on.

All good things come to those who wait.

One weekend, as I was travelling across the UK, on my way to London to see my family, I got an email. It was an email from the owner of the newly branded 'Mess Around' and the subject line said: "Franchise for sale." Her territory was suddenly available! It was a sign from the Universe telling me to go for it, so that's exactly what I did. I fired back an email immediately and told her that absolutely,

I was interested. My future, my career, my life as a Children's Activity Provider began.

I joined the 'Mess Around' family because I wanted to be part of something special. Being a first-time mum can be a lonely experience, as I eluded too earlier. I had left my family and friends to go live on the West coast of Scotland, (a story for another day), but after only one year, we moved back south to the Midlands and once again my other half went off to work, all day, every day. I craved the opportunity to work, and I wanted to work with someone like-minded and to feel part of something. With 'Mess Around' I had reconnected with my purpose. I had a career and best of all, it was one that I could build around my family while giving other children and their parents a truly memorable experience.

You'll notice I seem to be making a big deal about 'My Why', like it's a matter of life and death. That's because it is, from the perspective of your business at least. So, what's the big deal? Why do you need a purpose? Well, it's easy. Starting, building, and successfully running a business, is a veritable rollercoaster ride of emotions. You have your ups, and you will have your downs, and it's your purpose that will get you through the tough days.

You will have days when you wake up wanting to quit, to jack it all in and get a 'proper job'. You'll compare yourself to your friends and neighbours who seem utterly content with the 9 to 5 and always seem to be going on holiday, or spending quality time with their kids, while you're busting your butt trying to make a sale. And there will be days, when the presentation, that you've been rehearsing with your child for the last week, is about to kick off at school and you're going to miss it because you've got a class to run, or something else has come up. You will sit and wonder why you're doing what you're doing and think to yourself that maybe you've got it all wrong.

I tell my clients to have their 'why' printed out and displayed somewhere they see it every single day, to remind them why they started their business, why they are at their laptops late at night, and why they missed the school play.

Let your 'why' carry you like a ship through the turbulent seas ahead.

So, I'll ask you again. What's your why? What's your purpose?

Mission

Tom Cruise had a mission, albeit an impossible one. He always knew what his target was and why. He also knew when he needed to achieve his goals.

Your business, like every other business has a purpose, a reason for why it exists here on planet earth. It has a mission. So, what is it?

My mission as a franchisor was to bring fun and laughter to the children of the world. With my current online business, it is to make business education accessible to all.

Your mission statement doesn't have to be long; a simple sentence will do.

Vision

Now that we have our mission clear, let's move on to find out about your hopes and dreams. What are your business ambitions? Where do you want to take your business? As a franchisor, for me it was:

"To be the number one and largest messy play provider in the UK."

My dream was to see children at our events in villages, towns, and cities across the UK.

That was the vision that led us to franchise the model in 2012 and to subsequently create a subscription box in 2017 so that children could experience the magic of what we had created.

At the beginning of your entrepreneurial journey, you get to dream big. It's your chance to scope out your plans before you get lost in the day to day running of your business.

So, use the Chapter Challenge and list down all of your ambitions for the business you are creating.

For those of you aren't already clear on your vision, it's time to do it now. It's never too late to think big, but it does get harder to think outside the box.

Values

We know your business mission, we've discussed your vision, but deep down, what are you all about? What do you want people to feel when they think of you?

Values are what drive your business activities, they guide you in your decision-making processes and support your staff to achieve your business goals, whether you employ, franchise or license, you need to have your values in place, otherwise you will get steered off course.

Values help you to build loyalty with your customers. We had six key customer facing values when I was a franchisor:

- Family fun,
- Exploring creativity,
- Making memories,
- Bonding time and Friendship,
- Sparking imaginations,
- Providing the ultimate sensory experience

And our business facing values were:

- Honesty
- Integrity
- Fun
- Customer Satisfaction
- Ethics
- Teamwork
- Imagination and Creativity

These values underpinned everything we did at 'Mess Around'.

I want you to think about what your business values are, customer facing and business facing. We will need them when we get to the implementation stage.

Goals and Milestones

Without objectives it's difficult to measure your success, so let's be clear on your goals. Whether you're building a car or a house or a business, you need to have a plan, a series of milestones/goals that you need to achieve by a certain time. A plan not only shows where you're going, but also whether you're going to get there and if you're going to get there on time. Done properly, a plan will help you determine your critical path to success; by helping you highlight what dependencies exist between tasks and milestones, and therefore what blockers there might be up ahead. Discovering that there is a potential roadblock up ahead now, will help you ensure you can get around it easily when the time comes.

So where do you see your business in 10 years' time, what do you want it to look like?

I know this may seem such a long time away and even with a mission statement and a vision in the bag, you may have no idea what the business will look like in 10 years' time, but you need to dig deep. Your vision is what you need to work backwards from when we get to the planning stage.

Going back to when I was a franchisor, my end goal was to have one hundred franchises across the UK, with millions of children attending our events. I wanted a full team at head office managing operations and I was aiming to be focussing full time on international development, if that pesky covid hadn't got in the way.

So, my goals were clear. I had milestones associated with the number of franchisees I needed to bring into the business and by when. Milestones for when I would need to expand my website. Milestones for awards, and clear targets for launching outside of the UK. I had target dates for new product launches and more or less, a route for getting me where I needed to go.

For my current business I'm working towards developing an 'Agency' business model. I intend to have a team in place managing the core business and I have a target date for relocating to Spain. The sub plan in that, being my daughter's Mermaid Swim School.

That may seem a little over the top to many, but we have a business mapped out for my youngest daughter for when she finishes school. It's a 10-year plan and together we are developing the plan now so that we can make it happen.

My daughter has recently been formally diagnosed with severe Dyslexia. Although she is making fantastic progress, the chances are that academia will not feature highly in her future, so we are stacking her knowledge now. We are giving her valuable life skills so she will have more options later. Or in other words, equipping her with the tools that she will need to run a successful business, and right now, she has her heart set on teaching children to swim, mermaid style.

But enough about me, let's get back to your goals. Start with what the business will look like in ten years' time and then reverse engineer it until you're down to year one. If it's easier, break it down into short, medium, and long-term goals.

It's this goal setting work that will form the basis of your business strategy.

Strategy

Right, we have our why, we know why we exist. We have a defined mission statement, a vision, values, and business goals. Now we need the strategy to help realise our ambition.

If you enjoy planning, this is totally going to be your bag. You need a plan, in the words of Monica Geller, you need a jam plan! A prospective client recently said to me:

"I want to work with you, but I see you're so busy and have a lot of programmes that you're delivering right now and I'm worried that you won't be able to give my business its full attention."

This did make me chuckle. It's not often I get a question that gives me the opportunity to reply with a personal anecdote that also references my product. I replied with:

"I'm pleased that you have noticed this. Yes, I am busy, but you don't need to worry. I have a business strategy with a marketing and sales plan that I'm executing, which is enabling me to hit my targets for this year, getting me one step closer to my ten-year goal."

OK, so what's my point? Having a strategy is what you need if you're going to achieve your ten-year vision. I've said it before and I'll keep on saying it: Business is a marathon, not a sprint. I'm talking Paula Radcliff not Usain Bolt.

In 2022, I ran my first marathon. I had decided at the beginning of the year to set myself a personal goal and I had heard that running a marathon teaches you a lot about yourself. I was going through menopause at the time and my hormones were sending me crazy; I needed a focus, something to get me through this period. (Little did I know I actually needed a bucket full of HRT, but I'll tell you all about that later in the book.) Back to the marathon and my point, you would not stand on the start line to run a marathon without doing the necessary training or having a plan for the event. It would just be plain silly. At best a waste of time, at worst you could seriously damage your long-term health.

Some people will train for up to a year for a marathon, or if you're like me, train for ten months. I've been running since the age of nine, so I have a lot of miles in the tank, but I still would not run a marathon without preparing for it. I followed a training plan, I took advice on fuelling for the race, I set myself short term goals by entering races in the build up to the marathon. I had my family dropping me off miles away from home for training runs. I made sure I had all the right equipment for the big day, from trainers to good fuel, a water bottle that didn't leak and clothes that didn't chafe. Most importantly I tested my body and my equipment as I went along to measure my performance. I pushed myself out of my comfort zone and ran 20-mile stretches well before the big day.

My point is that if you're going to launch a business, why would you not have a strategy? You've heard it before: Failure to plan is a plan to fail. Too many people go into business with a short-term view and do what I call 'bob along' - I actually recorded a Podcast on this - Start, Grow & Scale, Episode, Are you ready for 2024? Of course, it's ok if you're a bobber and you have no need or intention of pushing the boat out, but I will assume, given that you're reading this book, that you're not a bobber because clearly you have at the very least, a desire to increase your knowledge of marketing.

There are also those that launch a business, with full tilt entrepreneurial energy, but they fall at the first hurdle, because they simply hadn't thought it all through.

If you want big things for your business, then you need strategy.

You need a plan!

Simply put; to build a successful business you need a strategy. Once you have a plan, people need to know about your stuff and to let them know about your stuff you must be visible. In order to make sales, people need to know, like and trust you and so, building a personal must be your priority. Marketing Like A Pop Star will help you to build that personal brand, just like I have.

I see business owners who struggle with marketing and don't want to be visible, because they have imposter syndrome. I know this to be true as I have been there too. When I launched my online business, one of the reasons I created the Children's Activity Business Club was because it was a product, something that I could hide behind. I had imposter syndrome big time. My partner and I discussed this at length, should this business be Kristine Monaghan, or should it be the Children's Activity Business Club? I had my doubts, who was going to buy from me? I worried that people within the sector were going to say, "Who's she to put herself out there as an expert?" This was in fact utter nonsense going on in my head, stories I was telling myself, due to menopausal anxiety, and was completely untrue. However, at that time it was easier to hide behind the product; I did until I realised that if I wanted the Children's Activity Business Club to be the business I envisioned in ten years' time, I *had* to build a strong personal brand. It was this personal brand that would become integral to my business foundation.

Chapter Challenge

Explain your ***WHY.*** What is the driving force behind your business? What is your purpose?

Write a simple statement that explains your mission. What is it that you aim to achieve in your business?

Now think about your vision – what dream do you have for your business?

Now think about your values... both customer facing and business facing

Customer values	Business values

What are your goals and milestones?

1 year

2 years

3 years

5 years

10 years

"Get closer than ever to your customer. So close in fact, that you can tell them what they need, well before they realise it themselves."

Steve Jobs

RULE 2

Know Your Customers

Who do you serve?

You have no business if you have no customers, it's as simple as that. Customers are the lifeblood of your business. If you want customers, then you need to be clear on who you serve.

When I became a franchisor in 2013, I had next to no idea about franchising or messy play. However, I had amassed considerable experience from my former life in sport, coaching and management, which had given me the fundamental skills that I needed, to grow my new business. I was not from a teaching and education background, so I knew nothing about the benefits of messy play, but as a parent and customer, I knew it was a fantastic activity to do with my daughter, and that's all that mattered.

Back then, the 'Mess Around' business model was to run weekly term-time classes that would cater for 12-15 children for 45 minutes at a time. Remember I said I had left Skye and had moved to the Midlands, well less than two years later, and five days after the birth of my second daughter, we decided to move back to Skye. This time I was fortunate enough to be able to take a franchise with me.

On Skye, there were no 'Children's Activity' classes as such. We had play groups in village halls dotted around the island. Entry was £2 and the children ran around a hall generally entertaining themselves, while us sleep-deprived parents ate cake, drank tea, and chatted about the antics of island life.

10 years ago, there was little chance that parents on the island were going to pay £5 per child for a weekly term time activity. Added to this issue, was the fact that I now had two children to feed, water and give my undying attention and love to; weekly classes were not going to work for me anymore. If I wanted to continue with my business, I had to think out of the box. One day, while strolling up to the Fairy Pools with my eldest daughter, my youngest strapped to her father's chest, I had an epiphany. I decided to host a messy play *event* instead of a class. On that day, the future of 'Mess Around' was born.

Events, I could run every four weeks, or stagger locations throughout the month. It meant less work and more money, so I went for it. Six weeks after I had given birth, I was hosting my first messy play event in Kyleakin hall. My aim was to get as many people as possible through the doors for £5 per child; it was the only way I could make the business viable.

Having set up my messy play area, which looked like a giant patch work quilt, I was ready to host my first event, and host it I did. Over 70 children and their parents, travelling from every corner of the island, came to 'Mess Around' that day. For over an hour, parents, grandparents, uncles, and aunties, all got messy with the kids and had fun. It was fantastic. The atmosphere was completely different to my weekly classes back in the Midlands; it had a party vibe. Everyone was chatting, laughing, smiling, making new friends, and having fun.

The cherry on the cake was the feedback I received that day. It was amazing. People were already asking me when the next event was going to be and right then, in that moment, I knew I was on to something. My customers were not only parents with children. Whole families wanted to have fun. It was that very event that kickstarted the generation and evolution of 'Mess Around's' core values, and it was crystal clear who we served. Our customers did not come to our events so that their children could learn and be taught, they came to us because they wanted to have fun. They wanted to be entertained. 'Mess Around' was an entertainment business.

As the business grew, we began to narrow down on who our ideal customer was. This meant that we were able to increase our ability to target the right people more efficiently through our marketing. I can't stress enough how important this is! If you want to attract a crowd, your content must speak to them. To use one of my partner's fishing analogies: 'To catch a certain kind of fish, you need a certain kind of bait, and to stand any kind of chance of catching those fish, you need to fish in the right pool, or more simply put, you won't catch a salmon, in a pond, with a worm!'

Once you have your messaging right, and you're telling the right people, in order to keep those people interested, you must, must, must, must, remain consistent. Stick to your values. Stick to what you know.

In this way, 'Mess Around' was built around my perfect customer. It was built around parents who wanted to see their child entertained, and to be surrounded by happy smiley faces. If one of my franchisees started posting about the benefits of messy play, they would be reminded that they were going off brand. There were other providers who were in the business of educating children and the virtues of experimenting with food. We were not one of them and it was my job as the Director of the business, to make that clear. I was there to carve out a niche and to position ourselves in the children's activity field, as a purple cow, standing proud amongst the herd of black and white ones. It was my job to make customers know that we were different, and that's what I did.

I did it by having clear messaging. I did not talk about education, I talked about fun. If people wanted their children to learn something in class, other than how to have fun through messy play, then they went elsewhere. Don't misunderstand here, I was well aware of the benefits of messy play. Time after time, parents would feedback saying how our classes had utterly transformed their child's absolute aversion to certain foods. Picky eaters would become less so. I even had adults that had started to crave mushy peas after a lifetime of revulsion. Children with sensory processing difficulties also did spectacularly well. It was wonderful to watch the expressions on a child's face, as their toes squidged in the bright green spaghetti or when they sank their hands into a tray of slime. To this day I still take a huge amount of pride in the children our classes helped, but that wasn't our business goal. I've said it before, and I'll say it again, "We were there to entertain."

So where am I going with this? To be clear, understanding who you serve is vital if you want to build a successful business. It doesn't mean you're not going to attract people who are not your ideal customer, but it means you can aim your messaging directly at them, and I'll talk more about why that is important, later.

Let's make sure you know who you serve before we move onto the next step.

What do you do?

Are you a service provider or a product-based business? This may seem a strange question to ask - it's pretty obvious right? Well, maybe not. I've seen so many business owners start with one idea but before they know it, success shines, and their little idea grows and spins off new and more exciting ideas, it's the nature of business. It's very easy to get carried away and to lose sight of where you started, and where you were going.

It's part of being an entrepreneur. It's why we are all in the game. Got to get bigger, better, faster, stronger. Sometimes the desire to achieve more, can lead you down avenues you hadn't planned for, and if you haven't planned for it, then failure is a risk.

I've done it myself with 'Mess Around'. We were a service providing business, through and through and our mission was clear. However, I then created a product called The Mess Box. The Mess Box was a subscription box, created just when the idea of subscription boxes was taking off. It was pretty awesome if I say so myself. But I wasn't finished there. Soon after I created a programme called Slime Lab UK, which was incredibly well received. This I topped off with the MessBeRaver, a large messy play rave for children and adults. Glow sticks and UV paint galore. They were some seriously fun times.

These were all great businesses. The only snag was that I didn't have the infrastructure in place to support all four simultaneously. They were essentially four separate businesses, which needed individual leadership. I recognised this and had to make some tough decisions on how they would be managed in the future. I needed to make sure that I didn't lose sight of my mission, which was to get to 100 franchisees.

The reason I'm talking about this is because you must one hundred percent stand behind your service or product and the transformation it provides when you're building a personal brand. This is what you will be talking about in your marketing.

So, now is the time to review your business activities and rank them in order of profitability and priority...this will help you to identify where your priorities should lie and whether these priorities are in line with who you serve (your ideal customer) and your visions and goals. There should be a synergy between all the stages of the strategy planning – of things look to be 'at odds' with other parts of your overall vision or mission then you may need to make some tough decisions – remember if you lose sight of your goals, you run the risk of drifting and losing focus.

What problem do you solve?

We all have problems that need solving...

- You can't spend time with the kids because you have to work.
- You can't get your dogs out every day because you're working, so you need a dog walker, or
- You waste your precious time, cleaning your house when you could be working on your business, and a cleaner would help to buy your time back.

Yesterday I lost an hour of my time, food shopping and I said to my daughter, "We need to start getting our shopping delivered to the house again.", I can't afford to lose the time or money; every time I go shopping with my daughter, she always wants a new toy!

Right, now we have what you do and the customer you serve, we're going to look at how you solve your customer's problems with your service or product.

Mess Around's solution was that we provided fun family entertainment; and this was straightforward. With my current business, which is predominantly an online business, I've had to do a lot of work around my ideal customer, figuring out what their pain points were, and their biggest one was **time**. Specifically, the lack of it. They're parents juggling a business with parenthood, and with this in mind I built my services around giving them their time back.

My message is simple, be clear on what problem your business solves. Even if you're just starting out or you've been in business for some time, go back and review what problems your business solves; we will be using this in our marketing when we get onto building our personal presence.

Transformation

Let's be real, people want to see results from your services or the products you offer. They want to see a transformation, either in themselves or in their child, family, or friends. If your service says you will teach a child how to write their name in six weeks, then you need to make that happen or show what progress they have made in that period. If you're telling the world your product will make life better by solving a problem or meeting a need - whether it's a piece of code, an electrical component, a language class or a mess play event - you need to come up with the goods.

People want to see what they have got for their money; it really is as simple as that. If you say in 12 weeks, your client will have lost a stone in weight and will look and feel better, (providing the client does the work), then you need to demonstrate that transformation. The same principles apply to all businesses. You want to deliver an exceptional service or product that gives results, and you need to show that to your audience.

With my sports business, parents wanted to see that their child's skills were progressing. I taught Javelin, Discuss, Shot Put, Running and Coordination and through, it parents wanted to see their children's confidence grow. They wanted to see that their child was learning something new and that they were happy. By the end of a six-week course, parents could see the transformation in their child, which is why I was always fully booked.

If you have an online business, then you must show your clients' transformations to your audience. Without it, it will be much harder to build the 'Know, Like, Trust' factor.

It took me a significant amount of time to really define what my audience wanted from my business. However, as I dug into the wants and needs of my ideal customer, it became apparent to me that generally, their biggest desire was simple. They wanted to make more sales. Service providers want to be fully booked and product sellers want to sell more products.

My clients come and work with me because they have a problem that needs solving and through my clear messaging, I'm able to demonstrate how I can help them.

I show the transformation of my clients. How I take them from A to B. This wins me business every single day.

Chapter Challenge

Let's get to know your ideal customer...

Who is your Ideal Customer? Write as much detail as possible. Remember this is the ideal customer - who you would love to have in your business?

Write down what problems you solve for your ideal customer. What are their pains and challenges?

What's the transformation your services/ products provide for your ideal customer.

"Don't be a rotten Strawberry."

Jenni Dunman

RULE 3

Adopt a Success Mindset

Believe in yourself and your brand or believe in yourself and your brand. There are no other options.

Over the past 11 years I've worn many hats. I've been Coach Krissy, a Sports Manager, a Charity Director, a Franchisor, Miss Mess, The Queen of Slime, The Small but Feisty Business Coach, Children's Activity Business Expert, and now a Marketing & Sales Expert, and whichever hat I have worn, I have worn it with pride and protected it at all costs.

Over my years as a franchisor, I awarded over 70 franchises and built a strong and visible network across the UK. I launched a Subscription box, one of the first of its kind, and a subsidiary business called The Slime Lab. I even tried my hand at directing and producing a YouTube channel called Mess Around TV. My Facebook page grew to over 22,000 followers, and across the network we had over 100,000 followers. Over 50,000 parents were on our email list and thousands of children participated in our events across 200 locations in the UK. The brand was in exceptional shape and ready to scale.

On the downside, many people copied us. Competitors even used my legal documents and photographs to launch and promote their businesses. Even though, as they say, all is fair in love and war, it still took me a while to eventually see the funny side of my branded floor mats in photos apparently taken in competitor's classes, (there was even a high street national store, constantly using one of my franchisee's photos), or Mess Around Ltd. mentioned in the T&Cs on a competitor's sales page, but as I've always said:

You can't beat the market leader, by copying the market leader!

Back then, if you had cut me in half, rainbows of goo, slime, green spaghetti and glitter would have spilled out of me. That's how strong my belief was in Mess Around. I lived and breathed it. Whenever I set up a class, it was a reflection of me. Every tray, every material, every mat represented me and the brand, and people could see it. The effort that I put into my classes was clear and it made all the difference. People copied the layout, but they couldn't copy me.

My point is this: you need to be 100% behind your brand. Business is hard. There are always ups and downs. It's much easier to stand behind a product when the product isn't you, but if you don't believe in yourself, if you don't believe you are worth the investment of other people's time and money, if you don't believe you can make a difference in somebody's life and fill a hole, then nobody else will. I make it sound easy, but it's not. In a society filled with doubt, training your brain takes time; you must work on your mindset every single day.

I don't claim to be a business psychologist or a mindset guru, but I've picked up a few things along the way that I'm going to share with you; tips on what I do to train my brain to build that success mindset. You must develop your brain, just like you would develop your body. Heading back to my marathon story for a moment, when I started to increase the mileage towards the end of my training plan, I threw in a few runs that were 18-22 miles long, to get my body ready for running for a long period of time. "So what?" you may ask, "You were running a marathon after all." True. How can I put this in a way that's easy to understand? It's not actually the distance that hurts, at least not for me. I knew I was fit enough. For me, my marathon, the hill I had to climb, was the amount of time that I was going to be spending on my feet. I didn't need to train my lungs and muscles as much as I needed to train my brain, to accept and cope with the pain that would soon manifest in my feet.

There's a reason they call it hitting the wall. When our body reaches a certain point, when it's been pushed to its limits, it feels like you literally do hit a wall. You can't go on; you can't get past. The tank is empty, you've burnt up all the fumes, and with it, all your resolve. Knowing this, I ran those long distances repeatedly to make myself believe that, if I could run at least 22 miles in training, then I would find the extra four miles from somewhere. I would get through the wall.

Repetition, repetition, repetition. Do enough reps, and it gets easier. You must train your brain to rinse and repeat and push past that pain. Be it pain from a marathon, or the pain of running your business, you must go all in if you want to see results. That's why mindset really does matter.

For what it's worth, if you really want to test yourself mentally and physically, a marathon is the way to do it. It's hard, make no mistake, but the rewards are exceptional. You'll feel like there is nothing you can't do when you cross the finish line, except perhaps stand up and maybe talk coherently.

The marathon that I had chosen to test myself with, was the Inverness marathon. It is the most scenic marathon in the UK, but what I hadn't appreciated during my repeated virtual runs along the route in Google maps, was how undulating the course actually was; not great for a fast time or first marathon. The race started and off I went with hundreds of other runners, my playlist locked and loaded, inspirational music filling my ears, and my tank chocked full of slow-release, high octane fuel. The race started well. My mile times were respectable and on pace, but by the time I hit mile 10, my thighs had started to sing louder than my playlist. They were in some serious fatigue, which for the life of me I couldn't understand. I had not had any inkling of this pain in training. I continued with the race, but when I got to mile 15 the pain really started to kick in and by mile 20, I was in a mess, my own little private world of pain.

Here's the thing: I had told myself that I was going to run this whole marathon and that walking, was not an option. This was the only marathon I ever planned to do. But here I was, my legs screaming and my brain telling me that this was more painful than giving birth, (at least when I was giving birth, they gave me drugs).

Out on the road, in the middle of nowhere, there were no drugs, in fact there were no runners either. I was stuck in what they call no man's land; no runners in front of me and no runners behind me to push me through the race.

It was just me and my mind monkeys, who by this stage were having an absolute field day. "Stop and walk! You're hurting yourself!" On repeat. The pain that I was feeling was so bad that the monkeys even started trying to convince me that I was putting my health at risk; that I could drop dead, leaving my family behind, my children motherless, and for what? A run around Scotland! It sounds extreme

I know, but this is the subconscious I'm talking about. That weird place where everything is real, working at its finest… but I pushed through.

Truth be told, it was seeing my family at the end of the race that got me through. I won the argument and beat the mind monkeys. I convinced them that I wasn't going to die. *"I won't walk, I'll be ok, I will finish this race, my family will be proud of me."* I wanted to show my two girls you can do anything you want if you put your mind to it, and this is what I told myself, on repeat, until I got to the finish line. I hobbled across the line in 4 hours and 59 minutes, in tears, vowing never to do that again!

Guess what? I did it again a year later.

Self-talk

The moral of the story was that it was my mindset and self-talk - the voice with which I answered my demons - that got me through the day, that, and the utter belief that I could run a marathon. I apply these same principles to my business now. Every time I must do something out of my comfort zone, like climb up on stage and talk to a large crowd, I give myself a pep talk and remind myself of marathon day. That if I can run a marathon, then I can do anything. I've trained my brain to handle the nerves and switched my nerves to excitement. It's because of this that my body reacts to stress in a different way. I've trained my brain with positive affirmation. Instead of being scared to go on stage I've flipped it to say I'm excited to get on stage and share my knowledge. I can't wait to be able to see everyone

I highly recommend following Mel Robbins, whose podcast I listen to. Mel is an American podcast host, author, motivational speaker, and former lawyer. She is known for her TEDx talk, "How to Stop Screwing Yourself Over"; and her books, The 5 Second Rule and The High 5 Habit, as well as host of The Mel Robbins Podcast

She's all about how to tame our self-talk. Go listen!

Positive affirmations

I have worked hard on my mindset over the last two years and let me tell you, it's not easy, it takes practise. Just like brushing my teeth and washing my face, I have built into my daily routine, attending to my mind. So, when my teeth are clean and my face is dry, I rebalance my thoughts. My mindset activities have become part of my life.

I confess, the idea of working on myself, my attitude and my mental health, is relatively new to me. I've grown up around people and in a generation where self-doubt is considered a weakness and something not to be talked about, and it seems I'm not the only one.

Putting this into a business context, you may be surprised to learn that a huge percentage of business owners suffer from imposter syndrome. The eternal doubters, who no matter how long they have been doing what they do, a part of them is waiting every day for somebody to come up behind them, tap them on the shoulder and declare, "You're a fake!"

When I started building my personal brand, many moons ago, I was a doubter too. My mind monkeys would frequently keep me up at night by tap dancing on my shoulders, just as I was falling asleep, relentlessly questioning me:

- "Who are you to say you're an expert?"
- "Who are you to be saying you're the best?"

- "Who are you to say you know about building a personal brand?"

It took me quite a while to shut those monkeys up, and it took effort.

Before I go to sleep every night, although it sounds strange writing it down for the first time, I 'practice' gratitude by telling myself three good things that have happened to me today. Even if it's been the worst day ever, I find three things that I'm grateful for. It's even rubbed off on my youngest daughter, who finds it useful to help her wind down at the end of the day.

And it doesn't stop there: When I'm in the shower I tell myself that today is going to be a good day because...

- I will be helping my clients to move their business forward
- That one more business owner is going to have the confidence to action
- That I am a magnet for sales

and that:

People want to come and work with me because...

- I'm passionate about getting them results
- Of my energy
- I speak the truth
- I have a no-nonsense approach
- I empower them
- I build their confidence
- I'm fun

This is the work you must do if you want to build a successful personal brand.

Figure out what positive affirmations you need to build into your day.

Testimonials

Get them up on a notice board, on your fridge, on the inside of your wardrobe, where you can see them every single day. Not only are testimonials and reviews important when building your personal brand, but they also support you to build a success mindset.

Running a business is a roller coaster of emotions, some days you're on cloud nine and then on other days, you're down in the sewers with the rats wondering why the hell you started your business in the first place. It's these days that you circle back to your why and purpose.

Read those testimonials and reviews to reflect on why your work is important and how you're making a difference to others in your world.

So, get the printer out, go and download all those testimonials and reviews and get them printed off and display them proudly where you can see them every day.

Surround yourself with the right people

This is one of the most important things that I have learned in business:

Surround yourself with the right people.

They say you are a combination of the five people that you spend the most time with, so if you're spending your time with the wrong people, then I truly believe this can affect your success.

If you want to be a successful business owner, then you need to spend most of your time with successful entrepreneurs, other business owners who are ahead of you in the game.

If someone is ahead of you and is making more money than you, then it is likely that they know more than you simply through having spent more time in the game of business. It means you may have something to learn from them.

You want to surround yourself with people who will push you to head out of your comfort zone. People who will drive you on to the next level of success. That's why I love my business club. It's full of the right people who want to have a successful business, who are prepared to learn and do the work. It's also why I'm part of a Mastermind, so I can have the right people around me, cheerleading me from the sidelines.

Running a business can be a lonely experience, so it's important to get the people part right.

Rotten Strawberries

Which brings me nicely onto Rotten Strawberries; I love this quote from my friend Jenni Dunmore.

"Don't be a rotten strawberry, and don't surround yourself with rotten strawberries either."

As you know you only need one rotten strawberry in your punnet to turn the rest green and mouldy. Negativity is contagious and it breeds like wildfire, which is why I cut all the whingers, whiners and naysaying nellies out of my life when I started to build my personal brand, including friends.

The complainers who reliably complain on Facebook, or the canvassers that ask for advice but don't take it (unless it's what they want to hear), people who moan about you behind people's backs or people who generally don't have anything nice things to say about anyone, have all gone from my life. I suggest you do the same.

These people distract you from achieving your goals and dreams and just zap your energy, so start a culling and get rid. Stop following them on Facebook and Instagram and cut them from your life.

You need the right people in your life, protect your circle at all costs.

The Universe

You get what you give.

I've never considered myself a particularly spiritual person, and I'm not going to start chanting now, but consider for a moment the number of adages there are regarding giving:

> *"No one has ever become poor from giving." - Anne Frank*
>
> *"We make a living by what we get. We make a life by what we give." - Winston Churchill*
>
> *"The meaning of life is to find your gift. The purpose of life is to give it away." - Pablo Picasso*

> *"Service to others is the rent you pay for your room here on earth." - Mohammed Ali*

> *"We know only too well that what we are doing is nothing more than a drop in the ocean. But if the drop were not there, the ocean would be missing something." - Mother Teresa*

> *"He who wishes to secure the good of others has already secured his own." – Confucius*

> *"No act of kindness, no matter how small, is ever wasted." - Aesop*

Yes, I know we are all in it to make money, we are in business after all, but I always try to treat my customers the way I would like to be treated, with kindness and respect. Sometimes it is hard, but it is always worth it, and generally the Universe will respond in kind; it's a state of mind.

It took me a long while to figure out that your mindset matters when it comes to business, and I recommend that you work on yours every single day if you want to be unstoppable.

Chapter Challenge

Practice positive affirmations. - What affirmations will you use to work on your positive mindset? Write some ideas here...

Now Print off your testimonials and reviews and put them somewhere you can see them every day.

Finally, do an audit of who you are spending your time with and choose only the people who motivate and inspire you and who bring positivity to your life.

"If someone offers you an amazing opportunity and you're not sure how to do it – say yes and you can learn to do it later."

Richard Branson

RULE 4

Get your messaging right

Show up every single day, a purple cow in a field of black and whites. Be somewhere, anywhere, ideally SEVEN different places every day. Get in front of your perfect customer!

That's the most important thing.

However, if you're not clear on who you are targeting or who you want to work with, your messaging will be wishy washy. You won't attract the right people because you won't be in front of the right people. You will end up in front of the wrong people, the ones who don't get you. They won't understand what you're about, the effort you're putting in, or what you can do for them. They will say that you're irrelevant, that you're spam, or that you're just too expensive. If your marketing is not targeted correctly, these people will fill up your feedback, your socials, your email and ultimately your mind.

We saw it in 'Mess Around' too. Occasionally some parents would randomly comment on our social media with things like, "That's expensive for messy play." Or, "There are too many people there, I don't like big crowds." So, we tightened up our messaging and made extra effort to get the value of what we provided and how we provided it, across in our content. I see it all the time with my clients today. Providers trying hard to grow and succeed, and the trolls who like nothing more than to pull them down. It's a sad fact about the internet, that with the unprecedented advertising and visibility it gives us as business owners, it gives an equal and perhaps greater opportunity to the haters, the mindless masses that like nothing better than to criticise and ridicule others, with the impunity that an internet connection provides.

I spend a lot of my time educating my audience about the need to know the identity of the ideal customer. Being clear from the outset is essential when marketing like a pop star and building your personal presence.

We were very clear with 'Mess Around'. Our target audience was a parent, a mum, looking for a fun activity to do with their child or family. As I said earlier, we weren't about education. If a parent wanted their child to learn mark-making, then they went elsewhere. If they wanted a morning of fun, that they could do with their friends and their family and at the same time make memories, then they came to us and they did, in their thousands.

That was the message that we put out in a big way. Through our branding, our live videos, our copy, the festivals, the events, the emails, the website, we sent it. Everything we did oozed that message.

Being on brand is essential if you want to stand out from the crowd and be noticed and recognised.

If you run a business, and especially if you are your brand, then you must be clear on who you want to work with. It is very easy to get over ambitions, or to simply get carried away with the excitement of launching your own business; even I sometimes make mistakes. For example, at the beginning of my latest business journey, I caught myself using language like:

"Calling all Children's Activity Providers!"

No, no, no! It wasn't long before I was painfully reminded that I did not want to work with everyone. So, I narrowed down my messaging even further into the niche and changed my messaging to:

"Calling all Action Takers, business owners who are SERIOUS about GROWTH, business owners who are prepared to invest in themselves and their business."

This soon got rid of the time wasters. There are an awful lot of people who want to own a business without having to work to make it successful. People that simply want you to do everything for them and want you to do it for free! I don't have time for these people.

If you haven't used ChatGPT yet, I strongly recommend you start. When you consider the astronomical number of questions and answers that have ping ponged their way through the internet every day, who wouldn't want to tap into the heart of it? Gone are the days of digging through the first website that pops out of an internet search, to find the answer you need, while blindly assuming that the website was written by somebody that knew what they were talking about.

ChatGPT, and other apps like it, are a new breed of search engine that use artificial intelligence, to give a more refined answer to your question. With the inherent training it gets from millions of questions every day, it's currently my tool of choice to help me really get inside the mind of my ideal customer. To help me understand what keeps them awake at night, what they worry about, what problems they are facing right now. Using it has helped me to get my messaging clear and in the process has helped me make money.

I regularly run training workshops and it always amazes me when I ask the question, "Who is using ChatGPT as a tool to save them time and effort?" And only one or two people raise their hands. I cannot stress this enough: these tools are **FREE** and are readily available, and at your fingertips, to assist you to optimise your work. Use them!

I'll be covering this more in Chapter 10.

Until then, understand that getting your messaging right, starts with being a big purple cow. This cow does not want to blend in. It doesn't want to look like all of the other black and white cows. This cow has something to say.

"LOOK AT ME!"

To be seen, you must define what makes you different from everyone else out there and emphasise that selling point. What is it that makes your product better? Why should people give their hard-earned money to you and not your competitors? It's noisy out there and it's getting noisier every day. Everyone is vying for our attention and it's not just your direct competitors. Apart from the multitude of businesses in your sector, filling Instagram with content, or the squillions of other accounts, filling your feed with eye candy, there are gaming apps, social media, email and the news also vying for your attention. Netflix, Amazon and Google don't want your customers to look at your adverts. They are spending millions making sure that your customers are looking at theirs. You have to fight to be seen. In today's world of instant gratification and miniscule attention spans, you have just three seconds to stop the scroll, so don't blend in.

When everyone is zigging, get zagging!

Personal Brand

Building a personal brand is different to building a company brand, but just as vital. Your company brand is primarily about the product and how good the business is. However, when you begin to build your personal brand, your target is trust. It's about building the know, like and trust factor with your audience so that they see you as the expert in your niche. Not only do you have a product that they want, but they have you, the trusted expert, behind the product, endorsing the product.

To achieve this level of interaction and relationship, you need to consistently deliver value until you become the authority. It starts with you shining the spotlight on the things that your ideal customers value. Show your customer that you understand their pain, show that you understand the marketplace, show that you understand the pitfalls and challenges and show how they can be overcome and then ultimately how you have overcome them, for your customer.

Once you have built trust with your audience, it's only then that you can really start to share how your products and services help them. Whether you're selling language classes or lawnmowers, portraits or consultancy, your audience is more likely to buy from you if they can relate to you.

My audience relates to me, because I've been in their shoes and walked the same journey as them.

This is how I did it with my current audience: I started being visible in January 2021 and did not ask for my first sale until May 2021. For five months I showed up on my socials, every single day with content that I knew would resonate with my audience. I talked about the things that I knew they cared about and every single Friday, I hosted a live session on Facebook to talk about a certain topic, such as "Why you need to use email marketing in your business."

I wrote blog content for my website based on those weekly lives, and I created lead magnets such as a free PDF with Top Tips, in exchange for an email address. *I cannot stress enough the importance of building an email list.*

I launched a Podcast called Start, Grow & Scale Your Children's Activity Business with the aim of delivering more content, but in an audio format. I knew my audience consumed content in different ways and they were generally time poor, so they listened on the go in between their classes or the school run.

For five months, I just showed up with value on the socials, in their inbox, online, and through partnerships.

I used my Market Like A Pop Star system that I'm sharing with you in this book to build my audience and to gain trust. I then began to promote and sell the system to my audience in May 2021.

It takes time and patience to build an audience of ideal customers; you got to aim to play the long game. This isn't the X Factor, no fame or fortune here in six weeks.

If you want to measure your success as a promoter of your own business, the one metric you need to track is your email list. Too many business owners don't have an email list. They make the mistake of building their whole business around social media followers and when the Universe decides to take it away, they are stuffed. We saw this last year when there was a Facebook outage. Everyone without a robust email list panicked; they had instantly lost their followers. The forward thinkers, who had invested time and money in building an email list were fine, didn't miss a beat. They were out making money, selling to their customers who were scrolling through their emails, getting their content and social fix.

Getting back to developing your personal brand, it takes time. You must lay the foundations first. I want you to think about what content you are currently talking about across your socials, in your emails and blogs. Look at what value it's adding to your audience's world and is it planting seeds for the future, when you ask for the sale? It needs to be content that matters to your audience. If it's not, then it's time to change up your messaging.

What do you want to be known for?

So, we've talked about becoming the authority in your niche, so now let's talk about what you want to be known for. When I first started this business, I was known for being the person knowing all things about marketing, but here's the thing, I wouldn't say I am a marketing expert. I know how to market a business, because I've learnt on the job, by doing it for twelve years. I know what steps you need to take to market a business and get results and although I love it, I never had any ambition to be known as an expert in it.

I wanted to be known as a business expert within my niche, as there was more to me than marketing. My services covered start-ups, growth, right to franchising a business model, so it was business expert positioning that I was looking for. This positioning didn't happen overnight; it's taken over a year to get my messaging right. I've worked hard on my pitch, so people know exactly what I do.

I want to be able to confidently introduce myself in any networking situation and for people to know who I am and what I do. If they didn't know me before, I want them to remember me and therefore be able to introduce me to others.

My pitch goes something like this depending on what I'm doing.

I help parent-led business owners to Start, Grow & Scale their Business by Unlocking their Potential, to maximise their income, so they get to do what they love.

This pitch links to the stages of my business services, plus my superpower and my audience's pain point. It's snappy, easy to say out loud and impactful.

Let's quickly talk about your superpowers. These are the things that set you apart from others, the things that no one else can do like you; your strengths. They are the things that other people praise when they are talking about you. So, if you're not sure what your superpower is, go and check out your testimonials and reviews and see what wording and language your customers are using.

If you see a common theme, then bingo! That's your superpower. Now we need to get your superpower into your messaging.

My superpower is the ability to see things that my clients couldn't see. I am able to quickly look at a business and see the potential opportunities that are open to them, that they are unable to see. I am able to discover ways to help my clients make money and to address their pain points, allowing them to do more of what they love.

Over time I have adapted my messaging to include my superpower and to address my clients' pain points. It's this messaging that I put out into the world to attract the right people into my business. It goes out in all my marketing, and it's aimed directly at my ideal customer, the bullseye person that I want to bring into my world.

What do you stand for?

Remember we looked at your business values, now it's time to look at what you stand for. Why? Because we will use this as one of our pillars of content when we start building our personal brand. People buy from people they know, like and trust, so you need to show what you are passionate about. If you're an anti-bullying ambassador, then you show this in your content. If you're passionate about ethical franchising like me, then that's what we talk about. If you want your services to be accessible for low-income families, then bang the drum about it.

When building a personal brand, you must be authentic. People will spot a fraud a million miles away, so don't pretend to be something you are not. These are the things that end up holding you back. When I started, I thought I needed to wear make-up, be seen to be wearing nice clothes, show that I was doing fancy things to build my business online, but I wasn't living that life; that's not me. I don't wear makeup unless it's a special occasion. I'm usually out running or cycling somewhere or walking my dogs on the beach, in the wind and rain.

So, I show up as the true me. A mum of two, a life partner to one, wearing a running kit or a woolly hat, living the dream on the Isle of Skye.

Don't get me wrong, if your life is about shopping, travelling, spending your day in spas, then show that in your content, if that's you. All I'm saying is show the true you, the person you are every day. Think about what you are most passionate about and get that into your messaging.

Make messaging your number 1 priority. What is your message? What do you want to be known for? What do you stand for? Use ChatGPT to help you get that message into eight words or less and then you have a solid message. Then aim this message at your bullseye customer – take the blurb that explains what you do and ask Chat GPT to shorten it into ten words or less and there you have your concise message!

Chapter Challenge

Now it's time to get your messaging right...

Firstly, audit your content and see if your messaging is clear.

Now write down what you want to be known for.

See if you can write down what you do in TEN words or less.

Finally write down, what do you stand for?

"I don't like to gamble, but if there's one thing I like to bet on, it's myself."

Beyonce Knowles

RULE 5

Show your credibility

You may not think it, but what you have done in the past, matters. Without knowing it, you are already equipped with a vast amount of material with which to market yourself.

A mistake that I see being repeated over and over again in business owners' marketing content, is a complete failure to include, and therefore sell, themselves. When creating an advertising profile and brand image, these budding entrepreneurs consider only their core business. They neglect to mention any of the interesting and relevant things that they have done and achieved in the past; their experience, their knowledge, their know-how, the things that they personally bring to the table. They are marketing their products and their services, but not themselves.

These business owners, and there are thousands of them, don't appreciate that to stand out from the crowd, you must lean into your past. You must explore what you know, collate it and share it with your audience. Display your credentials like medals of honour. Use your background to add credence and validity to everything you say about your business.

Your history highlights your value. It's your notable difference and it is this, that will set you apart from other businesses.

If however, you have taken on a business, whether it be a new franchise or a going concern, and you don't have the background in that particular field, (which is the route I originally chose with Mess Around), and you don't have that credibility piece that relates your experience to the business, then go back to you:

What is your Superpower?

What are you passionate about?

What do you love?

Why did you take on the business?

What's your motivation?

Lean into what makes you tick. Once you open the door to who you are, you will undoubtedly find a huge untapped resource of information. Nobody knows you better than you!

I use my creditability pieces in my marketing every day, to show my audience why they should work with me. What is it that makes me special? Why should they choose to work with me?

When I first became a franchisor, I had zero creditability in the pre-school world. I wasn't a teacher, and I wasn't a childcare expert. I wasn't an artist or an entertainer. I had only really ever worked in Athletics, but I had a superpower. My superpower was building systems.

I had spent a significant portion of my career to that point, designing processes and methodology with the primary aim of building meaningful bonds with children by engaging them through sport. I had also proved to myself that I was good with people. Being a city girl, and that city being London, it would have been impossibly hard to get through my childhood without interacting with people on a daily basis. I had grown up with people from all walks of life, and had trained hundreds of children, while I was still a child myself.

That's why franchising worked for me. As a franchisor I was able to tap into everything I had done throughout my life. I got to create and evolve systems and processes, I got to build teams. I got to engage children in new and interesting ways and set standards for how it should be done.

I also leaned into what parents said about us. Parents left our events raving about how much fun they had had. They shared photos and videos of their children and families on our social channels and publicly and privately recommended us to others. We used the reviews and testimonials from our customers, as yet another creditability piece.

Don't underestimate the power of your customer feedback. We all want to know what we are getting ourselves into. We want to know whether something is worth the money. We want to know whether we are going to be disappointed. We don't want to be fooled and taken advantage of. This is why reviews and testimonials are so important. How many times have you been asked for a review for a purchase of some kind, from house insurance through to a downloaded phone app? They want to know what you think. How often do you buy something via Amazon without checking the number of stars and the number of reviews it's had? Even if you don't read the reviews, it's good to know that people have been there before you and have literally already bought the T-shirt.

During my time working in Athletics with the National Governing Body England Athletics, the Olympic Champion, Jessica Ennis was one of our performance athletes.

It made sense to lean into that experience when I launched a Master Franchise in Scotland. The core business was teaching children the fundamentals of athletics and I knew that business like the back of my hand. As I mentioned earlier, I was already a level 3 endurance performance coach and I was able to use this as my creditability piece, to give parents the confidence in my business and the work we were doing across Scotland.

Fast forward to the present and now I do this every day with my current business. As often as possible I sell my experience and strengths:

- As a Franchisor with over 10 years of experience
- As a Master Franchisee
- As an independent
- That I've launched across the UK in villages, towns and cities across the UK.
- That I've helped business owners to franchise their own business.
- That I've launched a subscription box.
- That I've run an online business.

This puts me in a very strong position when I am working with my ideal clients. They know I have been in their shoes, that I've walked the same path as them and that I can short cut their pain.

What do other people say about you?

I love this question. What people say about you when you're not in the room is a reflection of you and your brand.

I once sat in a room full of somebody else's customers listening to the conversation. The previous week a business owner had come into the group to do a taster session for them. One of them asked another how the taster session had been. The response was not good; boy did she let it rip. The next minute they were all giving their opinion and let me tell you, they weren't good ones. I sat there quietly thinking, *"Blimey, I wonder what people say about me and my business when I'm not in the room."* I would have been devastated if that's how people felt about my brand. A friend of mine, who was part of the group, paused the conversation to tell everyone who I was and what business I owned. They then asked for my opinion. I gave my thoughts and turned the conversation around into a more positive one. I hadn't thought it was bad at all.

Regardless of the effort you're putting into your marketing, businesses can be made or ruined on your reputation and what people say about you. Word of mouth and recommendations are everything, and if the word of mouth isn't good, then you need to go back and look at the experience you're providing and get it right.

I learnt a lot from that conversation. It only takes a spark to start something smouldering under your business, and customers will spread a bad reputation faster than a forest fire. Sadly, a good reputation doesn't spread quite as fast.

Power of social proof

Reviews and testimonials are super important for brand building. You should aim to collect them on a regular basis. Not only do your customers buy your services as a result of friend referrals, but they will also seek you out based on recommendations. 9 out of 10 times this comes from online reviews and testimonials.

A prime example of this is an experience I had recently when looking to buy beds for my family. We had a spreadsheet on the go, and we were filling it with company details, pricing and delivery times, so that we could compare them and work out the best deal. We found one company that looked amazing. The price was fantastic, and the delivery options were perfect, but I had this nagging feeling that it was simply too good to be true. So off I went to see what other people had said about them on the company socials and reviews. Instantly it was clear that all wasn't as it seemed. When I landed on their Facebook page, there was a sea of angry face emojis. Every single post had an unhappy customer comment. As I read through the comments, I saw complaints about delivery times. Complaints about beds not actually arriving and refunds not being issued. When I got to the actual review, it got even worse.

Their customer service team must have been working 24/7 dealing with complaints.

That was enough for me. I wasn't parting with a single penny of my money. This was social proof at its finest. Whenever you ask for your customer to invest in your product or service, assume that they are going to check you out. They will want to know what other people have to say about you first, before making the decision to buy, so you need good social proof. It doesn't have to be all 5 star reviews, in fact a perfect record can also put people off but we need a good online report, that we can refer to in our marketing, if we are going to build a credibility piece for our personal brand.

Awards

When I first started out in business 10 years ago, I was not interested in Awards one bit. My business spoke for itself. The parent's stamp of approval was my award. My events were selling out month after month and so were my franchisees, so why did I need a strapline that said Award Winning? As far as I could see, awards were about the glitz and glam and there was no point in entering because I couldn't win anyway, I would have been up against the big brands who had hundreds of parents voting for them. So, I parked them to one side; truth be told, I've never been a glitz and glam kind of girl, so I wasn't fussed.

In 2015 however I was nominated by a customer for Most Outstanding Activity Leader for Under 5's in Northern Ireland & Scotland in the What's On For Kids awards[Lnk1]. Despite my view on awards, I confess it was a great feeling to be recognised publicly for all my hard work. Soon enough, the email came through, saying I'd been nominated, and I was given a digital badge to proudly display, but even then, and as much as it makes me cringe now, I didn't really do anything with it; gave thanks on my social media channels and moved on.

Then later that year, after much soul searching, I decided to bite the bullet and enter my first awards, the Mumpreneur 100[Lnk2], followed by Business Mum of the Year with The Family Network[Lnk3], at the time they were called Networking Mummies. Mumpreneur 100 was my first experience of completing an awards application which I then needed to submit to be judged. I didn't win, but I learnt a lot by completing the process.

In 2016 as well as entering the Family Network Awards for Business Growth of the Year, I also decided to Sponsor an award. I didn't have to complete any forms and being a sponsor would give me the PR coverage I needed at the time to raise the profile of the business; it was a win, win. I sponsored the Best National Pre-schooler Development award with What's On 4 Kids and the Flexible Business of the Year award with Working mums.

Looking back, these were three fantastic marketing opportunities for me and my business, but even though I made finalist at the Family Network Awards, and met lots of likeminded people as a sponsor, I yet again did not take full advantage of the opportunity in front of me. I just didn't appreciate the importance of entering awards and why they're great for business.

Over the next two years I learnt a lot about marketing. I had unexpectedly developed a real passion for it and to a certain extent it became my second career. Thankfully around then, I also started to realise the real benefits of entering awards. You see, it's not about the winning, it actually is about the taking part, as clichéd as it sounds. Just by entering an award your business is winning, in so many ways.

Or put it another way, who else is going to shout about you and your business if you don't? I often get feedback from clients who say they're not worthy of an award. That is utter rubbish, remember what I said earlier. I'll say it again. Awards are good for business.

I could wax lyrical all night about awards, but instead I'm going to get straight to the point and give you 15 reasons why you should not hesitate to enter one as soon as you can:

1. Awards give you FREE Marketing
2. Awards are good to build trust with your customers
3. Awards can help create brand loyalty
4. Awards help you to be recognised
5. Awards support your Search Engine Optimisation
6. Awards can be used in your content marketing
7. Awards give you an extra reason to email your customers
8. Awards attract franchisees
9. Awards are great for networking
10. Awards increase your credibility
11. Awards can be used in your competitor benchmarking
12. Awards can lead to more sales and more customers
13. Awards can help you to attract quality staff
14. Awards are a good learning process to go through
15. Awards are about celebrating success and are enjoyable

My advice is to throw your hat in the arena and get in there. You have nothing to lose. Just look at what I did in the last few years.

- 2024 – Club Hub UK –Winner for Supplier of the Year
- 2024 – Finalist for Service Provider of the Year
- 2023 - The Family Network Award - Winner for New Business Start Up of the Year
- 2023 – Business Success Network Awards Finalist for New Business Start Up of the Year
- 2023 – What's on 4 Kids Finalist for Game Changer Supplier of the Year
- 2023- Club Hub UK Finalist for Supplier of the Year
- 2022 – Sponsor of the Club Hub Awards: Leader of the Year
- 2021 – What's on 4 Kids: Most Loved Business Manager Scotland – Finalist
- 2020 – Club Hub: Franchise of the Year 2020 – Finalist

- 2019 - The Franchise Marketing Awards: Best Website - Finalist
- 2019 - Approved Franchise Association: Franchisor of the Year - Finalist
- 2019 - Best Business Women Awards: Best Franchisor - Finalist
- 2019 - What's On Awards: Most Loved Academic or Creative Activity - Finalist
- 2019 - Encouraging Women Into Franchising: Franchisor of the Year - Finalist
- 2019 - Elite Franchise: Top 100 Franchise - Finalist
- 2019 - The Family Network: Highly Commended for Business Growth of the Year
- 2019 - Sponsor of the Club Hub Awards: Young Entrepreneur of the Year
- 2019 - Club Hub Awards: Female Entrepreneur of the Year - Nominated
- 2018 - CV Magazine Franchise Awards: Best Children's Play Events Franchise - Winner
- 2016 - The Family Network: Business Growth of the Year - Nominated
- 2016 - Sponsor of the What's on for Kids: Best National Pre-schooler Development
- 2016 - Sponsor of the Working Mums: Flexible Business of the Year
- 2015 - What's on for Kids: Most Outstanding Activity Leader for Under 5's in Northern Ireland & Scotland - Nominated

If I can do it, so can you!

Chapter Challenge

What's your credibility?

List out your experience, knowledge and know-how.

What do people say about you?
Start collecting testimonials and reviews.

Find out what awards you could apply for and list them here...

"Show up – 80% of success is showing up."

Grant Cardone

RULE 6

Show Up

Consistency, consistency, consistency!

The key to success in my opinion is consistently showing up every single day in front of your ideal customer, even when you don't want to. It's not hard these days to show up; with so much tech available, you can automate everything you need to do easily. I teach my clients to use their day-to-day delivery or activity to market their business - for example, if you are a guest at an event, use this in your marketing, if you are testing a new product for your business, show this in your 'behind the scenes' marketing; everything you do, the way you run your business and your life, can become part of your marketing content. As time poor business owners who are juggling parenthood, this is the most effective way to get your marketing out there.

The consistency part just means what is consistent to *you* - if your consistency means post once a day, then post once a day and stick to it - above all, you **must** be consistent.

I have shown up twice a day on my socials for the past 12 years in all my businesses. If social media marketing is where most of your traffic comes from in terms of sales, then I say show up more, do more, do it better. Once you have that platform mastered you can move onto the next one - too many people try to master two or three platforms at once and do it poorly, spend time perfecting your marketing on one platform before you add more.

But here's the thing, you only need to show up where your bullseye customer is hanging out. That's the mistake I see many business owners making, they are trying to be everywhere when you don't have to be.

For me Facebook has always been my go-to social media platform, mainly because I've used it for so long. It feels like part of the furniture. I know how to build an audience, get engagement and how to monetise it.

Start where you feel comfortable. Don't start creating TikTok videos if you don't know how to use the platform, enjoy making video content or don't know how to use the TikTok platform effectively.

It takes time to learn a new skill, so spend that time learning, before you think about earning from that platform. If you don't know how to use it, then learn from someone else.

I'm a big believer in skill stacking, plus it saves you time in the long run if you're not having to learn it from scratch. If others have done the work, so learn from them.

If you have an engaged audience then they're waiting to hear from you, so why would you not show up? I will happily follow someone who shows up every single day if they're teaching me something or I'm finding out something about them as a person.

I show up every single day, in seven different places with my message, be it in an email, in the stories, a post in the timeline, or by doing a live video. You can take one piece of content, which I call a big topic i.e. a blog and break it down into multiple short pieces of content., then you want to get that same message out in lots of different formats. This is what I teach in my Market Like A Pop Star programme.

That's the thing to remember, people consume content in different ways. Some people love to read a blog, some people just watch reels, some consume stories for the highlights and some people like me listen to Podcasts. You will often find me getting my message out there in different formats as the brain processes information in different ways.

It has to be content that resonates with the audience though, which is also what I teach in the Market Like A Pop Star Programme. It can't just be any old content, it needs to speak to your ideal customer, so you grab their attention and stop the scroll. It needs to reward them for stopping, by giving them value, that way you will retain them as a follower and keep them coming back for more.

Do the things that other business owners aren't willing to do!

I tell this to my clients every single day. Do an analysis of your competitors' marketing, if they're not doing live video content, do live content, if they're not out delivering flyers in the area, then deliver flyers in the area. If you put the effort into the areas, where they're not showing up, then you will get the reward.

As an example of this, I hosted a roadshow series across the UK, so I could get out and meet more people face to face in small, personalised events, why? Because the industry that I service currently only has large one-off conference events, which not everyone can get to, due to the travel cost or time. They also don't allow for those real honest conversations that people need to have, so I created a Roadshow series across the UK to do the opposite of what these large conference events offer. I'm not about the glitz and glam of big events. I want to build meaningful relationships with people and the best way to do this is in smaller gatherings. Plus, I've also been fortunate enough to land a sponsor for these events, so they're now monetised. A win, win for me and my customer. So have a think about what you could do that your competitors are not doing.

Networking

This is where business is done, it's those in-person events, where you have conversations that lead to relationships and sales, so it's important to get out and about. You can network in many ways, online and offline. I personally prefer in person networking, as you can ask questions, learn more about your customers pain points, show them your personality and make those connections.

I know it can be scary to walk into a room full of people you don't know, I get it, I've been there, but the hardest part is making the first step. Take the first step and say,

"Right today I'm going to get out of my comfort zone and make the effort."

It's only that first step of walking into the room that makes you nervous, and remember, most people are feeling the same thing.

So, get out there networking today. Whether it's on the golf course, the squash court, a sales event canteen, or down the pub, go and meet your future clients.

Podcasting

I came across podcasts a few years ago when I was doing my weekly three-hour drive from the Isle of Skye to Oban to teach my athletics class. For 18 months I did that commute and although it's a beautiful commute from one part of the west coast of Scotland to another, across some stunning mountains and valleys, I was bored of listening to the same old music. I was constantly nagged by the feeling that I should be using my time better however, there isn't much you can do when you're driving. Holding a book and turning a page is quite difficult, especially when every ounce of concentration you have is focused on avoiding the deer, which love playing chicken with the unsuspecting driver first thing in the morning! So given that my hands and eyes were fully occupied on the task of survival, I decided to hand the responsibility over to my ears, and so my love of podcasts was born.

I kicked off my journey into other peoples' minds by listening to a podcast called "Feel Better - Live More", which was all about health and wellbeing. At the time I was suffering with some cracking peri-menopause symptoms, which I didn't know were peri-menopause symptoms, so I had been trying out various strategies for working on my mindset.

After gorging on that one, I came across another fantastic find. This one was about a guy called John McAvoy who had been sent to prison for armed robbery but then went on to become a World Record holder; I was obsessed. His story was amazing (he was an armed robber after all) and ironically, hugely inspirational. I raced through every single podcast with him talking about his life and journey. Sadly, it was over to soon.

This was how I was introduced to podcasting and I haven't looked back since. From then on, I ran through, and I am still running through every single podcast I can find on business from Diary of a CEO through to The Game with Alex Hormozi. I love podcasts.

So how did I get started recording my own podcasts?

When I started my current business, I began with what I knew. Blogging. I knew I needed to build my online presence and to begin showing my business authority. It's a busy arena, with lots of people all vying for the attention of prospective clients, and I needed to get back in the saddle, but I freely admit, I'm not a fan of writing. I find it much easier to talk about the things I know, than to hand craft chapter and verse, waxing lyrical with pen and paper (although it's much easier now with the birth of AI and tools like ChatGPT, but I'll come to that later), so I decided to record my first podcast.

I had had plenty of experience going live on Facebook and had spent a significant amount of time putting together my mini TV series on YouTube during lockdown, so I was fairly confident that I could make the switch. So armed with just my mobile phone, garage band and a podcast hosting platform I got started. It was rough around the edges, but it was something. I was taking action.

It would have been easy to get caught up with the idea that I needed all the tech, the bling, the jingles, fancy editing and audio production, and yes, at some point it is a necessary step in the evolution of a podcaster, but for me, I just wanted to get my message out there.

I kept my content short. I gave 30 minutes for interviews with clients, which I have decided is the perfect amount of time to allow a business owner to get their story across without the need for too much editing, and my topic of the day podcasts I kept to around 10. I knew my audience was time poor and like me, listening on the go. I also knew and they wanted practical tips, that they could immediately implement into their business, so that's what I talked about.

Just me and my phone, in the car. This from-the-hip style touched a chord, and my early podcasts were downloaded in their thousands!

It's brought so many people into my world, it helped me to nurture my audience, which has led to sales. What's more it led to a sponsorship with a major booking platform, all from one idea and taking messy action. You could do this too! Podcasting is a fantastic way to get in front of your audience. Don't let the fear of tech hold you back. Just get started and see where the journey takes you.

Guest speaking

Taking to the stage can be a scary prospect. I remember when I was asked to do my first guest speaking slot, which was at an awards event as a keynote speaker. The fear and nerves raced through my body when I was asked, but I knew I had to say yes. There was no choice as I was building my personal brand, and this was going to put me in front of an audience of 300 potential ideal customers. The other issue that kept me awake at night was that it was an hour slot! What was I going to talk about for a whole hour?

How was I going to keep the audience engaged for that long?

And to top it all off I was straight after lunch, the death slot, the time when everyone is fighting to stay awake in spite of a stomach full of sandwiches and tea cakes.

I'm all about creating a memorable, impactful experience, so people remember me. That's the aim of the game, to be remembered. You don't want to be remembered for being boring, or even worse, simply not remembered at all!

It's what I did with 'Mess Around' with our famous snowstorms, which was basically a giant foam party! With my sports business I created a Podium experience. This was no different. I was going to have to make my mark. I did what I always do, which is create that memorable experience.

I'm known for bringing the party and energy to events, so that's what I did, I got the crowd up dancing to the Venga Boys classic song: "We like to Party!"

Whenever I'm asked to guest speak, I think about how I can make an impact, how I can make people remember me. At one event I was asked to host the ice breaker, so I opened with a Greatest Showman theme. I gave every single person their own red top hat and I dressed up as a ringmaster.

I knew my audience loved props and would take photographs of themselves and their friends in these hats. I knew they would plaster the walls of social media with them, and they did in their hundreds. It got me more visibility. It got me followers and that day I was remembered. It was a marketing masterpiece, even if I say so myself.

I can't recommend guest speaking enough. It's a great way to build your personal brand, grow your audience and what's more you can get paid for it too!

When you have identified what's working well for you in terms of what is bringing leads into the business, be it your socials, podcasting or guest speaking, then this is where you need to amplify your message. Double down on it. If word of mouth is working well, think about how you can do more and do it better.

My Top Tips for Showing Up

1. At Mess Around we showed up in a big way through our events with live content on Facebook. We did the things other business owners weren't prepared to do by going live. Even now, I would say 90% of business owners are not using that free tool to get traction.

2. Showing up in reels. You don't have to be dancing etc. You could be creating education or documentary type content. Test what your audience likes and then do more. I love creating reels on Instagram, then sending an email to my list telling them to go and watch the reel. They watch that reel, this sends a signal to the algorithm that this is something interesting, which then in turns shows your message to more customers. I then download this reel and then post it across to Facebook and LinkedIn to get more eyes on that content. Use the free tools at your fingertips to your advantage.

3. Email marketing has always worked for me and my clients. There's money in your list. Email consistently with valuable content and the money will follow.

4. WhatsApp for Business is hot right now and it has some great functionality with stories, channels, broadcasts and groups. It's a great way to build relationships with your audience.

5. If I'm in a launch period, you can guarantee that I'm showing up at least three times a day on the social timeline if not more, in the stories, in your inbox, and I will do personal outreach. No stone is left unturned.

Chapter Challenge

Time to think about how you are showing up...

Review how consistent you are with your marketing - list the places and platforms you use and how often you show up; be honest!

Research and list the places where you could start networking

Explore podcasting - listen to some that inspire you and make notes on how it could fit in your business and whether it is for you.

Could you take to the stage? What opportunities exist for you either digitally or in person?

"In learning the art of storytelling by animation, I have discovered that language has an anatomy."

Walt Disney

RULE 7

Tell a Story

Facts tell, stories sell!

If you want to build yourself some personal presence and a recognisable and respected internet identity, then you need to be using storytelling in your marketing.

The human race has been telling stories for thousands of years. Much of history as we know it, has only survived because stories were passed from generation to generation, back before literacy was common and the idea of the internet would have gotten you stoned or burned as a witch.

Stories are a particularly powerful way of showing yourself to the world in order to influence others, or simply to find like-minded people; people that will respond to your message. When done well, it can provide an immersive and potentially participatory experience for the reader or viewer. With over 50 million novels having been written in English alone, and over a billion videos and movies being churned out across the world, it is clear that there are people out there that want to listen, they want to be taken out of their world and put into yours, even if just for moment.

I for one, am always telling stories. Whether it's a story about me and my experience, or that of a friend or a client, I enjoy that act of communication and expression. In truth, it all boils down to the fact that people buy from people that they know, like and trust and the quickest way to build that is through story telling.

There are many different ways that you could be using storytelling in your marketing, to make you stand out from the crowd, but fundamental to all of these is:

Talk about what you know.

I strongly advise against talking about stuff you know nothing about; people will see right through you. When I first became a franchisor, I had no clue about the benefits of messy play. There was no way I was going to be advertising how my classes were helping develop young minds without knowing all the facts, so I used what our customers said about us to create our content and leaned into that instead. I told my story, starting with my values, highlighting what I brought to the table and what I wanted my customers to get from their time with me.

Remember, no one has lived your life, so they can't tell your stories. This will always make you unique in the marketplace.

The following is an outline of how I approach my story writing. I suggest, when you are considering your next blog, your next video or your next advertising campaign, that you use this approach for determining the focus of your piece.

- Past Stories - These are the things you have done in the past. All of those experiences that make you, you. Think of your business then consider the world, consider society, consider the news and then relate it all back to something you know about.
  - Example:
    - How I delivered my product while eight months pregnant.
    - How I employed young people through my business to give them a sporting chance in life.
    - How I built a franchise network to 40 franchisees in five years.
    - How a global pandemic changed my life and what I learned from it to improve my offering.

- Recent Stories - These are the things that happened in the last month. Keep it topical. There is always something going on in the news, in your area, or in your industry.
  - Example:
    - Its 2024 and an Olympic year. Let's get ready!

- Trending - Look at what's currently trending, which isn't hard to do these days. You know X, you know Youtube, you know Instagram and TickTock. Think about how you can jump on that trend.
  - Example:
    - A quarter of children under seven own mobiles phones and they are missing out on the real world.
    - How my client made £35k in four weeks despite a growing cost of living crisis.

- Your Story - This is where you can get creative. Think of something relatable to your perfect customer. Something that potentially helps define who you are and what you're capable of.

There will be an infinite list of things you can write about that you have never considered worth sharing.

- Example:
- How I ran my business from a remote island out in the Atlantic, during the pandemic!
- Why I became a franchisor.
- The trials and tribulations of moving to the Isle of Lismore.
- Cockfighting on my croft.
- The day we got stuck at Carfest mudfest.

Putting this all into context, to help me get my new business rolling, I decided to take my audience on a journey; a journey of discovery if you will. I kicked off with a story about me, running my first marathon. I used video (vlogging) to show people behind the scenes of my training runs and races, in the build up to the event.

This approach meant I was able to build a rapport with my audience. By running a marathon in the first place, I inherently showed my audience that I could commit to training, that I had endurance, the mental strength and dedication necessary to see things through to the end. It showed me in many different lights and, so I've been told, provided a significant number of people with some much-needed inspiration.

My stories said many things, such as:

How much you want something is proportional to the effort you put in to get it.

The world is your oyster, but you have to work for it.

Put in the work and reap the rewards.

You get what you give.

Think about how you can take your audience on a journey with you.

Chapter Challenge

What stories can you share?

Past stories

Recent stories

Trending stories

"If you want to be successful, you've got to be willing to use every connection you've got."

Magic Johnson

RULE 8

Engage

Social media is about being sociable.

Don't be afraid to get involved in somebody else's story. Whether its Instagram or Facebook, TikTok or X, recognise to be recognised. If you want to build your personal presence and build it quickly, then start engaging in other people's content. Get involved in the discussion if you can. Show the world you have something positive to say and therefore something positive to offer. There is a good chance that an already ongoing and relevant discussion, that you know something about, involves your ideal customers. If it's related to what you do, and other people are engaged, then some of your work to find those people and draw them in, has already been done for you.

Better yet, if the originator of the story is discussing issues that you can help with, go for it. Whether you're selling a class, a course, a tub of slime or a car, offer your assistance whenever you can. Every positive contribution you make to another person's story, will inevitably lead to people looking for you, to find out who you are and what you do.

Remember, the internet can be a scary place. It's a global stage on which anybody can stand and say just about anything they want, about anything and anyone they want. In turn, that global stage comes with a global audience that is also free to say anything they want about anything they want and most importantly of course, about you and your business.

Understanding this is key to understanding why the vast majority of people who are willing to take the leap and stand in the spotlight, will be hugely grateful for your positive feedback.

So, once you understand who your ideal customers are, follow them online and engage with their content every single day to form and develop relationships. It must be meaningful engagement, not just a love and like on their post. Take the time to read their content and give your thoughts, opinion, and/or appreciation.

So that's your customer's social presence, what about yours?

When it comes to creating the content that you need for your ideal customer you must:

- Grab their attention,
- Speak to them in a language they understand,
- Be on brand
- Be aligned with your values.

This is how I've done it for the past 12 years and with it I have grown audiences of over 100,000 followers plus and have also made this a primary part of my Market Like A Pop Star Programme.

Clearly, I spend a lot of time online. I spend that time keeping up to date with latest trends and looking to see who is pushing boundaries and standing out from the crowd. I think it's fantastic when I see somebody doing something different, somebody that stops me scrolling through an infinite array of noise on Instagram. Sadly, those people are in the minority. For the majority, I see business owners putting out content that is boring and irrelevant. Often what they say is not even on brand or aligned with their values, which should be a shooting offence!

So, what do I mean by not being on brand? Most businesses look a particular way. Their core branding may have a particular colour scheme and a specific font. They may be vibrant and noisy, or cool and calm. They could be super casual, or elegant and high class, and it's all related to their core values. Whatever the strategy, for it to be effective, it should be consistent throughout their marketing. However, time and time again, I see social media for the sake of social media. It's painfully obvious when a business owner purchases one of those templated packs and tries to apply it to their work in their niche. It doesn't resonate with their customers because it's not on brand. It's not what they're meant to be about and therefore it's not what their customers are about.

The majority of what's online is simply too generic. Little to no effort has gone into creating content and the one size fits all approach does not work if you're not making it specific to your audience. If that sounds like you, then you're wasting your time.

Facebook Groups

Make no mistake, posting and running is spamming.

Don't post and run. Throwing something into a group in the hope that somebody is interested enough to come to you, without the courtesy of sticking around to engage about your post, will not make you friends, it's unlikely to be particularly successful either.

Select groups that are full of your ideal customers, visibly engaging in the community. Groups that are brimming with sales posts that no one is talking about, are not active groups and are a waste of your time.

Enter groups with the intention of being helpful, it's called breadcrumbing. Show up, scatter your breadcrumbs by answering questions and offering advice. Let people get comfortable with you; let them get to know you and where to find you.

One trick is to make sure your personal Facebook page is up to date with what you do. People are naturally inquisitive and when you start getting involved in conversations and helping people, many of them will automatically consider you an expert and they will check you out. They will go to your personal Facebook page and provided they like what they see, and it relates to the idea of you being an expert, they may start referring you to others and that's what we want.

When someone asks for a particular service in the group, we want people piping up on your behalf, saying how you are the best person to help them with that. Groups are a great way to build relationships. It takes time, but there is only one of you and more of them, so the more people that know about what you do, the better.

Communities

Be visible where your ideal customers hang out, and if you want to get known in the local area then get involved in community or niche events like conferences. There is nothing better than getting out and about in your local area, talking to your customers at the coalface. If you find there are no specific events for your niche, create your own.

Little tip... if you are going to attend community events or host your own, you need a way of collecting email addresses and mobile numbers, so you can engage with them after the event, so get a hook in place like a prize giveaway or a lead magnet. If they give you their contact details, they get to enter or get a discount code.

Do not just stand there like a lemon and do nothing to promote yourself. I've seen plenty of people do that at my business events in the past, you need to find a way to interact with people, give them a reason to come over to your stand, create a buzz, sell something so you make your stand money back! Use the opportunity to get content for your social media and email marketing, get the most out of the opportunity.

Partnerships

Partnerships are vital when building your personal presence, but don't choose just anybody or any organisation to partner up with. Choose wisely, be strategic!

I only work with organisations or people, where I can see a two-way mutual benefit for the both of us. More often than not, people will happily take your money but for very little in return. You may get some short-term advertising, but there is little longevity in it. What you need to start looking for are opportunities to build lasting relationships.

My relationship building started with me sponsoring Awards. As a sponsor, or win or lose as a nominee, they are a great way to get in front of your ideal customers, (assuming you pick the right awards), and to get exposure. Whether your field is children's activity or private education, online service provider or a bricks and mortar business, there's an awards ceremony that you should be engaging with.

However, when you're starting out, you are unlikely to have the funds to invest in every award going, so be strategic.

I only invest in people or organisations that are going to give me the most exposure, in terms of social media and marketing. When looking for partners, before I make an approach, I want to know the size of their email list and therefore their inherent outreach capabilities. Will there be speaking opportunities, website listings, photography and video content? This is where the payoff is when building a partnership. I avoid organisations that offer to let you send two emails or a blog per year, to their client list. They invariably ask for a big investment from you but offer very little in return. It's the nature of business. They don't have *your* interest at heart, they have their own. They want to make as much money as possible which means that giving you more for your money is not good for the books. On that basis alone, they're not getting my hard-earned cash.

Once you're up and running and you're forming solid business relationships, it's time to make those relationships work for you. It's time to start leveraging goodwill. Look for opportunities that allow each of you to market yourselves collaboratively. For example, if you have a great offer coming up, then you want your collaborator or partner to share this with their audience and to shout about you at full volume. Similarly, when your partner has something to share then you will return the favour. By marketing each other you are still getting exposure for your own business almost by default.

Conversations

Conversations lead to sales! If you want more sales, then you have to have more conversations. If you're not having a conversation every day, you need to do more talking. You should be allocating at least 30 minutes every day to starting or following up on a conversation with your ideal customer.

If you're feeling tongue-tied and need inspiration for calling out to potential customers to start a conversation with, simply start by asking some "yes" questions. Here are some examples I have used on social media:

- Do you want to make more sales?
- Are you looking to expand?
- Do you want to get fully booked consistently?
- Do you dream of having a waiting list of customers ready to buy your product?
- Are you looking to make £100k this year?
- Do you need a marketing and sales strategy?

Or how about:

- Are you looking for an affordable way to entertain your child?
- Do you want to sing like a pop star?
- Are you going on holiday and want a crash course in the language?
- Are you looking for a more affordable building material?
- Do you need a more robust design and development process?
- Do you want to know how to make your product robust?

These are all yes questions and the trick is to get your ideal customer nodding their head along with you. If you can do that and if you can get them to do that three times in a row, then you have them hooked.

We want leads to bubble up to the top, so start a conversation either via email or direct message (DMs). If you get a responsive customer, and your 'ask' is the right one, they are a great way to start conversations and make sales.

Treat your customers like royalty

Making a sale isn't the end of your relationship with your customer. Once you have made the sale and they're in your world, then treat them like royalty. They have just invested in you, your products and services, so you want to make sure that they feel loved. Treat your customers well and they will show their appreciation by coming back and buying more products. If they feel especially loved, they will tell their friends to come and knock on your door. If you have a product-based business, reward them for their loyalty via email marketing. If it's a service-based business, then loyalty cards work well and if you're running one to one or group programmes, check in with your clients to make sure they're ok, even after they have finished working with you.

It will pay in dividends in the long term.

Leverage your customers' goodwill

As a business owner it's vital to leverage the goodwill of our customers. We all have those amazing customers in our business, who comment on every single post, tell their friends about us, cheer, lead us on from the sidelines, buy more of our stuff... these are raving fans! If you are finding that new customers are hearing about you from word of mouth or friend referrals, then they are doing the heavy lifting on your behalf. We must remember that there is only one of you, and more of them, so the more raving fans we have out promoting our stuff the better.

Here's the thing... they're doing it for FREE, but the question is how could they refer you more and how could they do it better? Would they do more if you asked them directly by giving them a call to action at the end of your activities or if you gave them a paid incentive? Maybe through discount codes, money off coupons or extras like merchandise, or prize gifts? Once you have your raving fans, bringing in leads, then you have yourself, and a team of lead-getters, helping you to build your personal brand.

Chapter Challenge

Time to start engaging...

Be intentional about where you spend your time on social media. Make a note of the platforms and groups where you could start to spend your time strategically.

Pick 3-5 Facebook groups where you could start to build relationships.

Identify who you could work with as a partner...

Allocate some time to start Conversations on a daily basis – when will you do this?

Identify what customers are raving fans who could champion you

"Hard work will always bring opportunities."

Karen Brady

RULE 9

Perform

Your crowd is waiting for you to take to the stage. They want to devour your content, they want to hear what you have to say, they want to hear your stories, they want to know your values and what makes you different. They want to know why they should invest their time and money in you, so you must turn up and perform like the true pop star you are.

Just in case I didn't make that point clear enough, you must perform, but it's going to take work.

There is no getting away from the fact that you must do the work to build a personal brand; it takes time and lots of effort. If you're not prepared to do the work, then you won't get far. The success you dream of and tell yourself you deserve; you won't get without the effort. There is no short cut to success, business is not the X factor; fame and fortune are unlikely to be yours in six weeks. Some of you who have recognised that there are, in fact, no shortcuts to success, may head down the franchise business route, where the highs and lows of developing a product and refining all its attributes into a saleable asset, have already been done. The pain of business development, the trial-and-error rollercoaster, has ideally already been experienced by the franchisor. They should know what works and what doesn't, so that you don't have to figure it out yourself.

For the solopreneurs of you, you either take the plunge, learn on the fly and give yourself some permanent on the job training, or you invest in yourself and work with someone like me, a business coach or mentor, who is a few steps ahead of you and who can tell you how to prepare for what's coming.

That's the key, isn't it? You want to be a few steps ahead, and that's what a good mentor will be. Think of them as a version of yourself, jumping back through time, to tell you what you need to do to make you the success you are in the future. It worked for Bill and Ted!

But whichever route you take, you must be prepared to do the work, so that when you show up, you can perform at the top of your game.

You also need to practise patience. It takes time to build a successful, profitable business.

Go easy on yourself. Your sanity will thank you for it.

So, the key steps to performing better are:

Show how you add value

People want value from the content that they consume, otherwise they will scroll right past you, or even delete your email and leave you unread in the trash. There is an awful lot for your potential customer to choose from out there, so you need to be visibly worth their while, for them to stop for you. Don't be afraid to push the boundaries of what you think you know. There's no such thing as content being too long. People love to read interesting work. People want to know what other people think. What people don't like to do, is to waste time reading boring irrelevant tosh. Ask yourself, would you sit and read the stuff you are putting out there?

Keep in mind that people will binge watch hours of a Netflix series in one sitting. It provides an escape from the mundane; it adds value to their particular world for an hour or two. It gives them something to think about, or an excuse not to think. It's brain food one way or another. Now think about what you do with your content. If you're teaching your reader something or you share interesting and relevant stories that take them on a journey, or that connect and touch them in an emotional way, then they will show up, again and again and again to listen to you.

There are people today that I follow on social media. I eat up every little piece of content that they put out into my world, like I did with Madonna when I was a teen. There wasn't a thing she did, that I knew about, that I didn't engage with, in one way or another.

That's the thing when you create a piece of, "Look at me!" content for social media, or when you're neck-deep in writing your, "Listen to me!" emails. Think, "How does this add value to my ideal customer's life? Why should they care?"

And if you do that before you click the send or post button, it should give you an idea of what kind of reaction you're likely to get from your audience, and whether you should actually hit that button just yet.

Be Consistent

Another one of the big mistakes I see business owners making is their complete lack of consistency. As good as you may be, if you're sporadic with your marketing, and if there is no discernible pattern associated with when you show your face to your audience, how can you expect your audience to be ready to pay attention? You need people to be waiting for you to put out your next piece. You need to build expectations. For every business owner that doesn't make an effort to show up consistently and reliably, there are plenty that do.

Those who think, "I'll just post once this week, if I get the time, and my social media work will be complete" or, "People will engage with me, as long as I do something," will struggle. Unless you're Madonna, it really doesn't work that way. You must consistently show up every single day, delivering value like you mean it.

So, to start your drive to consistency, from your customer's perspective, you need to agree what targets you can stick too. From a private perspective, if your life will only allow you to show up once per day, then show up once per day and make sure you show up once per day, every day. Work out what blockers you need to remove to allow you to meet your consistency targets.

If you start seeing regular traffic coming in from your messaging and marketing, whether it be from your social media or your emails, then aim to do more.

"Strike while the iron is hot,"

"Make hay while the sun shines,"

"Get in while the going is good."

are just some of the many proverbs that are there to remind you to take advantage of the good times, and there is a lot of science and psychology in them too. It's much easier to give more, when you're getting more in return and feeling high on your success. Build on it when you can. Show up more in those places that work. Picture how your brand and your business will grow if you show up even more. In the early days, doubling your visibility and potentially with it your income, is easier than it sounds.

Being consistent is the key to success, and the people who are consistent, see better results for their business.

Implement a system

I'm all about systems, I just love them.

Systems and processes make running a business so much easier. Use them correctly and they become routine. As I have alluded to previously, my love for a structured approach to business is why franchising was a natural step for me and is also why I teach it in my business every single day. I built systems within systems during my time with England Athletics. I had built, implemented and proven systems across an entire county before I replicated those same systems nationally.

Those same principles apply to franchising, and to your business, whatever field it may be in.

For me, it starts with getting the foundations right, which is why we covered that at the start of this book. You must get the foundations dug first, before you even start to think of growing the business. Your foundations include: your marketing strategy, sales strategy, financial projections, tools and tech. Once those foundations are in, you can begin to add the walls and the rooms and the roof. Pretty soon you should have a solid business on solid foundations, that won't fall down with the first storm.

Creating a personal brand is like adding another room to the house.

Let's dive into the next chapter, where I will talk about the Tools of the Trade that can help you build that brand.

Chapter Challenge

How will you perform?
Write your commitment to perform here...

How is your content adding value to the world?

Look at your systems, review and note any changes or additions you will make.

"Never, set limits, go after your dreams. Don't be afraid to push boundaries."

Paula Radcliffe

RULE 10

Use what's available

As business owners we have so many free or low-cost tools available at our fingertips, that we can use to build our businesses. Getting started does not have to be complicated, in fact, it's quite simple. We just need to make full use of the tools we have before we move on to more advanced ones.

Here's my favourite 10 to get you started

Social Media

It's free, yet so many people don't use it to its full potential. Facebook has been my go-to platform for the past 12 years of business and I have built audiences of over 100,000 plus using Facebook for free. I've taught hundreds of business owners how to fully optimise the platform, by using all the free features that it gives you such as:

- Live video streaming
- Groups
- Reels
- Profile photos
- Banners

- Events
- And a whole host of Ninja tricks that can get you engagement, more reach and visibility and most importantly an audience of raving fans that will buy from you time and time again.

You've got:

- **Instagram**, which is another great platform, where you can build an audience, super-fast, if you post the right content.
- **LinkedIn** a platform that most business owners neglect, has upped its game, and it's now not just a place to look for a job.
- **Tiktok**, fast becoming the number one search engine platform, google watch out!
- **Threads** which has sprung up as an alternative to X as popularity declined when it changed from Twitter.
- **X** formerly known as Twitter for short form opinion content.
- **Pinterest**, yes Pinterest people! Is a social media platform that has great longevity for content, and don't forget,
- **YouTube** which is still one of the most watched platforms for video content and
- **YouTube Shorts**, their version of reels, is hot right now.

We have never had it so good!

There has never been a better time to start a business and it's never been so easy to build a personal brand than it is right now. New platforms are emerging every single day, and you could be on there, building an audience right now with zero cost, easily.

I get it, all these platforms can feel overwhelming. My advice is to start with one, learn it well, optimise it with your content, then move onto the next one. Don't waste time, trying to figure it out; PERFECTION IS THE ENEMY OF GOOD.

Statistically when it comes to learning new tools on your own, it will take you roughly 20% of your allocated time, to learn about 80% of what you need to know, but that last 20% of what you need to know, will take you 80% of your time to figure it out. You will never learn everything about the tool so don't try. You have too many other things to do.

For media like Instagram, my advice is that if you don't know how to use Instagram to its full potential, then buy a course or invest in someone who can teach you how to do it; there's plenty of people out there that can help you.

Email Marketing System

There are many email platforms that you can use for free out there to get you started, Mailerlite or Mailchimp are the main ones that spring to mind. Email marketing should form part of your overall marketing strategy and you should be list building as soon as you start your business.

Too many business owners rely solely on social media to communicate with their audience but here's the thing: You don't own your social media! If it's taken away from you like we have seen in recent Facebook outages, then you're stuffed!

Business owners who have worked to ensure that they have a robust email list are the ones making money when Meta goes down. When everybody else is on their knees, these entrepreneurs, simply turn to their email lists and they ping off their emails and keep their customers informed, and their business keeps rolling.

What I also love about email is that it can be one to one or one to many, therefore allowing you to make it personalised or generic as you see fit.

So, back to the point. When you first start out in business, you are unlikely to have a big mailing list, but that's not necessarily a bad thing. Yes, you ultimately want as big a list as you can get, but in the early days, it's at this time that you can really get to know your audience on a personal level. Take the time and the effort to hand craft your emails. Write the personalised ones. Make your customers feel valuable and needed. Let them know you 'see' them. Once your email list gets into the hundreds and thousands it becomes much harder to have those types of conversations. There are only so many hours in the day, but by then you will already have your brand out there and your tribe ready to receive your message.

I use my email list to build my personal brand, by telling stories and providing value, like giving out tips and advice to build my credibility piece.

When the time comes, you can monetise that list and begin to make money.

There's money in your list, so start emailing it today!

WhatsApp for Business

For a long time Whatsapp was a tool that I didn't really use; I'm a text message kind of girl. Then last year, after hearing how many people were using it, I downloaded the app and made a start of using it as a tool for my business. It didn't take me long before I switched to the WhatsApp For Business app. They've really stepped up their game. Whatsapp is no longer just a cheap way to send messages and photos. With the Whatsapp for Business platform there is a significant amount of stuff in there that you will undoubtedly find useful. This is just some of that stuff I mentioned:

- **Business Profile**: You can create your business profile and fill it with cool useful stuff for your customers, such as your address, business description, email, and website.
- **Business Messaging Tools**: You get tools like quick replies, away messages, and greeting messages to streamline your comms with your customers.
- **Labelling**: You can organise and even categorise your contacts or chats with labels to help you keep track of customer inquiries, orders, or any other relevant categories.
- **Automated Messages**: You can set up automated responses for frequently asked questions, which is a huge plus for your customer facing efficiency.
- **Analytics**: You get insights into message metrics, such as the number of messages sent, delivered, and read, so you can determine the effectiveness of your comms strategy.
- **Verified Business Badge**: You can get a verified badge to establish authenticity and credibility. It's ideal for getting your customers to trust your business.
- **Catalog**: You can showcase your products or services in a catalog to make it easier for customers to browse and make purchases.
- **WhatsApp Business API Integration**: You can integrate WhatsApp with your existing CRM system, helping you create reliable comms and data management across your other platforms.

- **Customer Support:** Although I haven't needed to use this yet, they provide customer support through real-time assistance, and it's all done directly through WhatsApp.

What I love about WhatsApp right now in 2024, is you can have quick conversations with your clients and potential clients very fast via voice notes, video notes, channels, statuses and lots more. As far as I am concerned, WhatsApp for business is a must have tool for business right now. Conversations lead to sales, and you can have them in WhatsApp.

But how does it help you to build a personal brand? Well, here's a few ideas:

- Just like email, you can get your message across with a Broadcast. You can create a list of your audience, with whom you can spread the word in style. The identities of individuals are kept private in a Broadcast. Think Blind Carbon Copy (BCC). Even if you have hundreds or thousands in your list when you Broadcast, like a BCC, the identities of everybody on the list are kept secret to each other; and you can reach your audience effortlessly. Try broadcasting a new blog, podcast episode, or a product update and see what happens. I like it a lot.
- I use their group chat quite regularly and it doesn't involve logging into Facebook. Use the Group Chat to build a community of champions. This allows you to create your very own private networking group, where people can come together to engage, connect, and grow. I love my WhatsApp groups.

- I also use the status updates. Just like stories on Instagram they disappear in 24 hours. It's a great way to keep your tribe on their toes and clued up about what you're planning.
- You can inject some personality into your "About" section. Share a fun fact or quote or something that makes you unique, so your business personality shines through.
- Lastly, use the AI features and get automated responses, so you can respond faster to your enquiries.

Manychat

This is a great piece of tech for automation for your business. You can build chatbots, automate customer conversations and engage prospects at scale. I love this tool and use it all the time in my business.

Scheduling Tools

An absolute must have. It's a time saver for you and the business and, as the name suggests, it means that you can schedule your social media posts over the coming days, weeks and even months ahead saving you time and having to post every day. It's great for when you know that you have a busy time coming up or you want to implement a series of strategic posts and messages. There are so many scheduling tools out there that you could use for your social media content. I always advise clients to use the most appropriate tool for their business, so if you just post content onto Facebook and Instagram then Metasuite will do the job, if you're posting in more places, then Buffer or Metricool are also great tools. I like scheduling tools as they keep you consistent and visible. I always have core content going out on my socials. It is however important to also have reactive content and engagement happening in addition to scheduled posts.

Canva

Unless you've been living under a rock, you must know about Canva. Millions of hours are saved every single day to this fantastic tool. For those of you that don't yet know what Canva is, think of it as your very own graphic design tool. With it you can create eye catching branding for your business at ease. It's a tool I use every single day to save me time and money. It has everything you will need from globally recognised, tried and tested templates, through to video content, stock images, the whole lot.

Mindmeister

If you're like me, you will have a million ideas going through your head at the same time... cue Mindmeister. A great tool for mapping out ideas and helping you understand your road map. When used correctly it will help show you the blockers and things you need to change to get where you want to go. I use it to create my course content, webinars, guest speaking talks, content, blogs. It's a great tool for drilling down and getting it all documented in one place.

ChatGPT

This new kid exploded onto the block in 2022 and hasn't looked back! It's one of a gang of tools that are going to change the face of the planet, only time will tell whether it's in a good way or not. It's a tool I use daily to help me thrash out ideas, come up with prompts, write my social media and email copy. I'm not a copywriter by nature, so having a tool like this, helps me in my day-to-day business. It saves me time and allows me to progress much faster.

When using ChatGPT, the key is to ensure that whatever you create with the tool, you then mould it into something that sounds like you. I don't recommend a cut and paste approach. Consider what it provides as a starting point, a partially painted canvas which you can complete with your own voice and the language style that you use every day and which your tribe will recognise as you.

Otterai

Another favourite of mine. I use Otterai all the time for transcribing my Podcast content. Combining the output of this tool and ChatGPT I can quickly create a blog and social media content that is based on the exact words I have already used, keeping my messaging consistent and sounding exactly like me. That might sound like a strange thing to say, but the fact is, that some days I am more me than others. Some days I'm on it, some days, for whatever the reason, I'm not quite there. Working smarter with these tools, means I don't have to work harder to achieve the feel I'm looking for.

Final Words

For anyone who has started a business before or thinking about starting one, the reality is you're going to face pain for the next two years of your life. No one said starting a business was easy, which is why 20% fail in the first year. The first couple of years in business is an uphill battle of building a brand, an audience, getting people to know about your stuff. It's one of the reasons why so many people join franchises, they want to short cut that pain as it's a tried and tested business model.

The fact is that you need to be tenacious, you have to have resilience and real clarity about your visions, goals and aims - you will not get to where you want to go if you don't know where you want to go in the first place!

With a clear strategy and by knowing what you want to provide and more importantly *who* you want to provide it for - aka your target audience - then you will be able to track your progress, measure the results you get from your efforts and refine and adapt your approach as you learn and grow.

Something that has really helped me over recent years especially, is that I've started to make a note of all the stories or things that I have learned over the course of each week from working with clients on a one-to-one basis or through my membership. This gives me real time content; the good stuff because it's happening right now. I then get this content out to my audience the following week, and the best thing of all is this content is going to resonate, as its coming from people just like them.

You should never run out of content ideas using this method and what's more your audience will know that you are in tune with them and what they're experiencing at the coalface.

When writing this book, I have tried to include the steps to success in easy-to-follow, bite-sized segments that I hope you will action and implement; remember nothing will happen without taking action, if there was such a thing as a magic wand, we would all be waving it!

Try to tackle the content one step at a time to avoid overwhelm. By working through the rules methodically, mastering each one in turn, you will soon see the results of your efforts as you build a brand that has a real and lasting impact.

Be the purple cow, stand out from the crowd and...

Market Like A Pop Star!

About the Author

Kristine Monaghan is a dynamic entrepreneur and author, originally from North London and now residing on the picturesque Isle of Skye on the west coast of Scotland. Partner to one and mother to two beautiful girls, Kristine's family also includes two beloved dachshunds.

Before embarking on her entrepreneurial journey, Kristine had a career in athletics development. This background laid the foundation for her disciplined and strategic approach to business.

Kristine has built and managed three multi-figure, award-winning businesses from the ground up. Her entrepreneurial journey began as a franchisor, where she spent nine years developing and expanding a messy play brand across the UK, growing a franchise network of 40 in just five years.

Demonstrating her resilience and innovative spirit, Kristine brought a new sports concept to Scotland as a master franchisee during the pandemic, which was no mean feat.

As a guest speaker and trainer, Kristine has educated franchise networks on marketing and sales, and has worked with clients to franchise their own businesses. She is the founder of the Children's Activity Business Club, an organisation dedicated to helping business owners unlock their potential to Start, Grow, and Scale their businesses.

In the past two years, she has worked with over 1,000 business owners, teaching innovative marketing strategies that drive success.

Now, she is expanding her expertise to assist online service business owners in building personal brands.
Kristine wrote this book to inspire and help others build a personal brand, a process she has successfully undertaken three times. Her clients inspire her every day to achieve more, and she is eager to share how others can get started with building their personal brands.

When not working on her businesses, Kristine enjoys staying active, whether at the gym or running marathons for fun.

Get in Touch

If you would like some help in your business journey, then I'd love to be a part of that journey you can get in touch with me in the following ways...

https://www.kristinemonaghan.online/MarketingSalesStrategist

QR code

Facebook

https://www.facebook.com/KrissyMonaghanSalesStrategist

Instagram

https://www.instagram.com/krissymonaghansalesstrategist

Testimonials

Client testimonials mean the world to me - they are the biggest compliment a client can pay to any business, and I value each and every one I receive.

I am lucky enough to have had far too many wonderful reviews to share all of them so here are just a few of my favourites - thank you all!

Abbie Ritson
Thank you so much for today **Krissy Monaghan** , i feel so privileged, attending your training session was nothing short of incredible. The day was an enriching experience, filled with valuable insights and it was fantastic to be able to apply it all immediately. What made it even more special was the opportunity to connect with fellow business owners who share the same passion and drive. I'm truly grateful for this learning opportunity and the chance to expand my network. Highly recommended!

Lindsay Murphy Top contributor
My mailing list is heading in the right direction - slowly but definitely surely!
My email campaigns have quite good open and click rates.
I'm getting way more interactions on social media.

I can see improvements and feel more positive about it this week.

Love Reply 1d

Rascals Theatre School
It looks sooooo beautiful!!! You are such an inspiration Krissy Monaghan!!! Anyone wondering whether this is right for you, let me tell you it is!!!! Krissy is amazing & not only helps you with getting your business on track but the community she has created is a massive support. Krissy has kept me going through what has been a difficult 6 months for me with a personal health issue & things are not able to move along as quickly as I had hoped but with Krissy's support I am able to keep going & keep chipping away on something that I may well have paused on completely. Thank you Krissy for being a massive support & inspiration, you really don't know how much you are helping me right now! Join the club, you won't regret it!!

4d Love Reply Hide 2

Rachel Elizabeth
I've had another good week. I've just generally had a much more positive mindset since the new year and that is all down to this club! I have a waiting list for a class that's fully booked so I'm going to add an extra class

Wendy Miller Coaching
Thank you for all of your support Krissy. You have kept me focused and motivated. I especially love the monthly coaching sessions and the resources you keep adding to the website just keep getting better! Joining you was one of the best business decisions I've made.

Pipsqueaks Performing Arts Parties & Classes
I am so touched by this mention...thank you so much! Since joining the 5 day Market Like A Popstar earlier in the year and then the CABC my mindset has changed, slowly but surely and now am seeing and experiencing a boost in my own confidence, self belief and income! Thank you Krissy, you're a bloody Star, a Pop Star!

Mini Mozarts North Wales
Aww, thanks so much for this Krissy Lovely post to come home to! And I cannot recommend you enough to other providers - if you're in need of a cheerleader, someone to hold your hand through a transition or just a kick up the bum, Krissy is your person!!!

Printed in Great Britain
by Amazon

44100088R00099